ABC Animal Coloring Book
ENCHANTED ALPHABET
from A to Z & exciting fairy tale

Educational Book for Toddlers and Kids Ages 3-6
with Interactive Learning, Fun Text,
and Easy & Simple Drawings to Color

Alexander Literansky

Hello, and welcome to

ABC Animal Coloring Book
Enchanted Alphabet from A to Z & Exciting Fairy Tale:

Educational Book for Toddlers and Kids Ages 3-6 with Interactive Learning, Fun Text, and Easy & Simple Drawings to Color

by **Alexander Literansky**

Copyright © 2025

All rights reserved. No part of this book may be reproduced, distributed, or transmitted in any form or by any means, including photocopying, recording, or other electronic or mechanical methods, without the author's or publisher's prior written permission.

THIS BOOK BELONGS TO:
_____

THE ADVENTURE BEGINS!

On a faraway island in the ocean lives a huge variety of animals. Here, strong eagles enjoy the fresh air and warm breeze, zebras and kangaroos hop across the green grass, lazy lemurs watch all the festivities from the trees, dolphins jump in the ocean, and crabs tease them from the shore.

Life was lively, and all the animals were very happy until a storm swept a wicked dark wizard named Pigmentikus to their island.

Pigmentikus didn't want everyone on the island to be happy; he was envious of the bright colors that nature had given the animals. Pigmentikus took out his magical orb and quietly muttered a spell. And immediately, rain began pouring from the sky.

The rain was warm, and all the animals happily ran out of their homes to enjoy it and splash in the puddles.

But oh, what a horror! When the rain stopped, the animals discovered all their bright colors had disappeared.

"Why are my wings not colorful anymore?" asked the butterfly.

"Who stole my beautiful red fur coat?" complained the fox.

"Why have my bright feathers become dull and gray now?" cried the parrot.

They had all turned black and white! Even those who were in the water were not spared.

Since then, there has been no laughter or fun on the island. No one is happy or playing anymore. No one jumps or swims.

And now only you can help the animals, my little friend!

Use your magic wands - colored pencils and markers - they will help bring color back to the animals!

A ANT

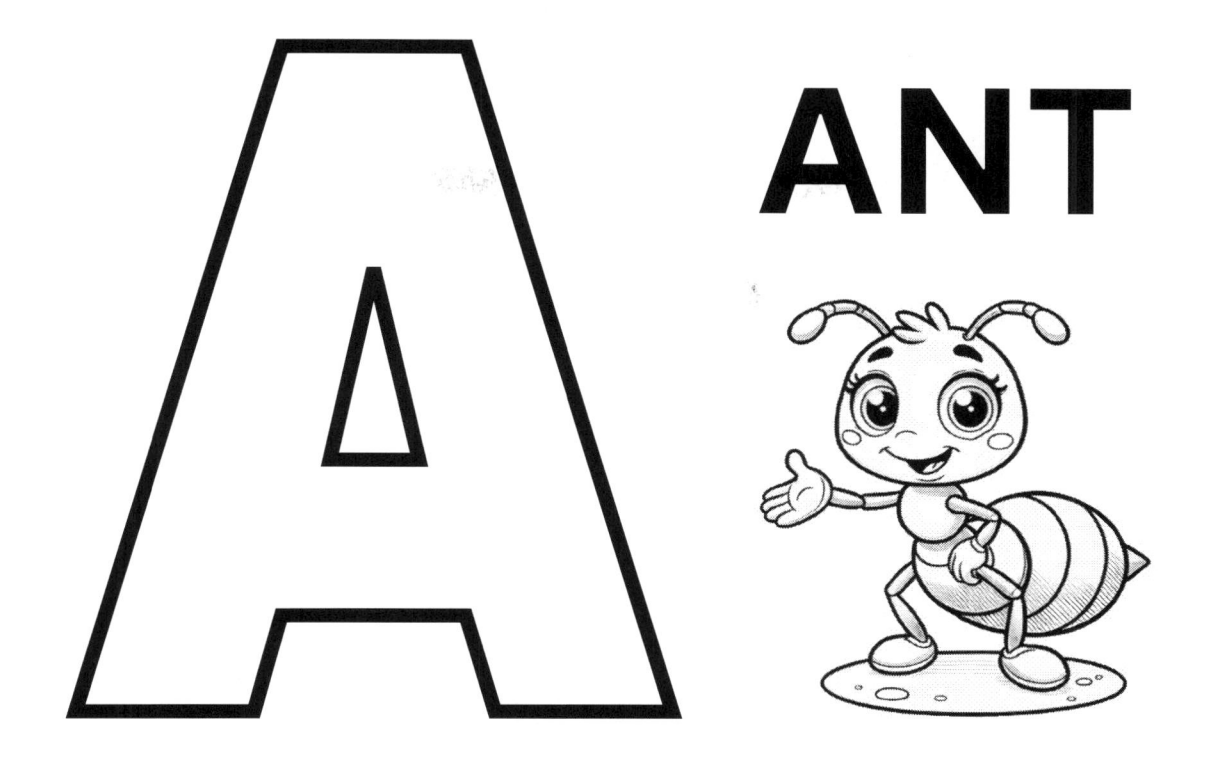

Ants are very smart and hardworking insects. They love to work together and help each other.

Did you know one ant can carry something 50 times heavier than itself?

That's like you lifting a car!

A

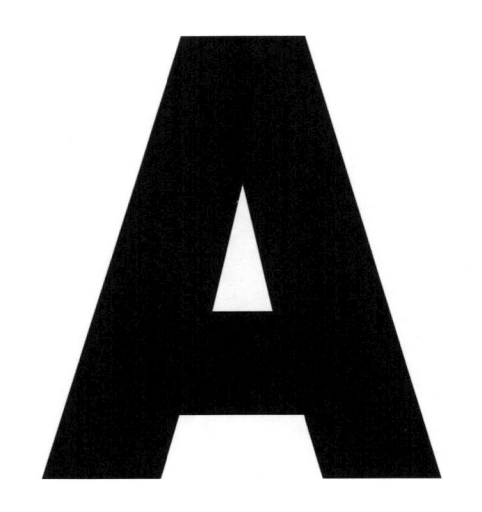

Okay, my little friend, let's write the letter 'A' together!
Are you ready?

A A A
_____

_____

Now you know what the letter A looks like, and you've learned how to write it.
Well done!

But I have a new game for you. The ant has come to visit us. He is very sad because he is all black and white. He really wants you to color him.

Will you help the ant become bright?

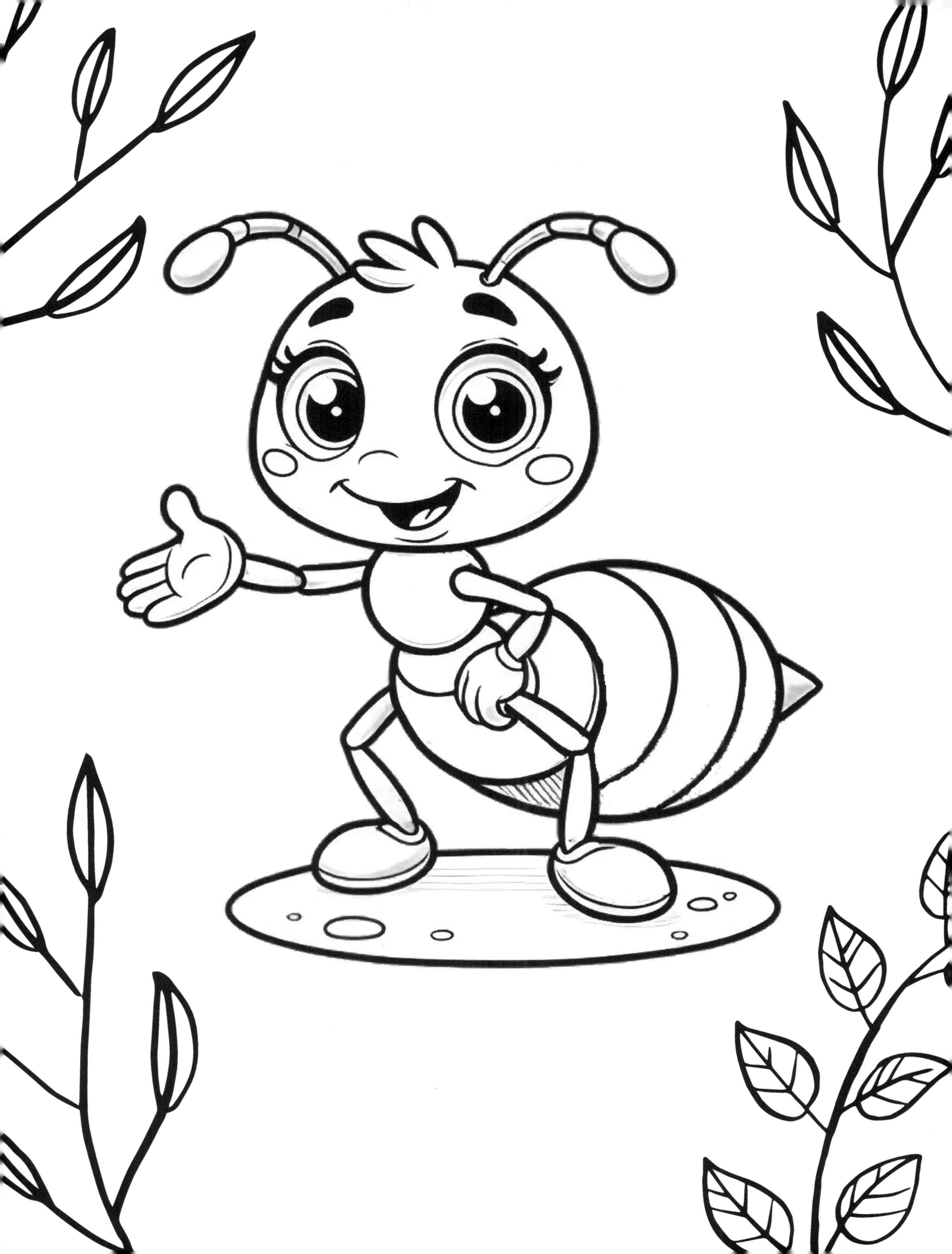

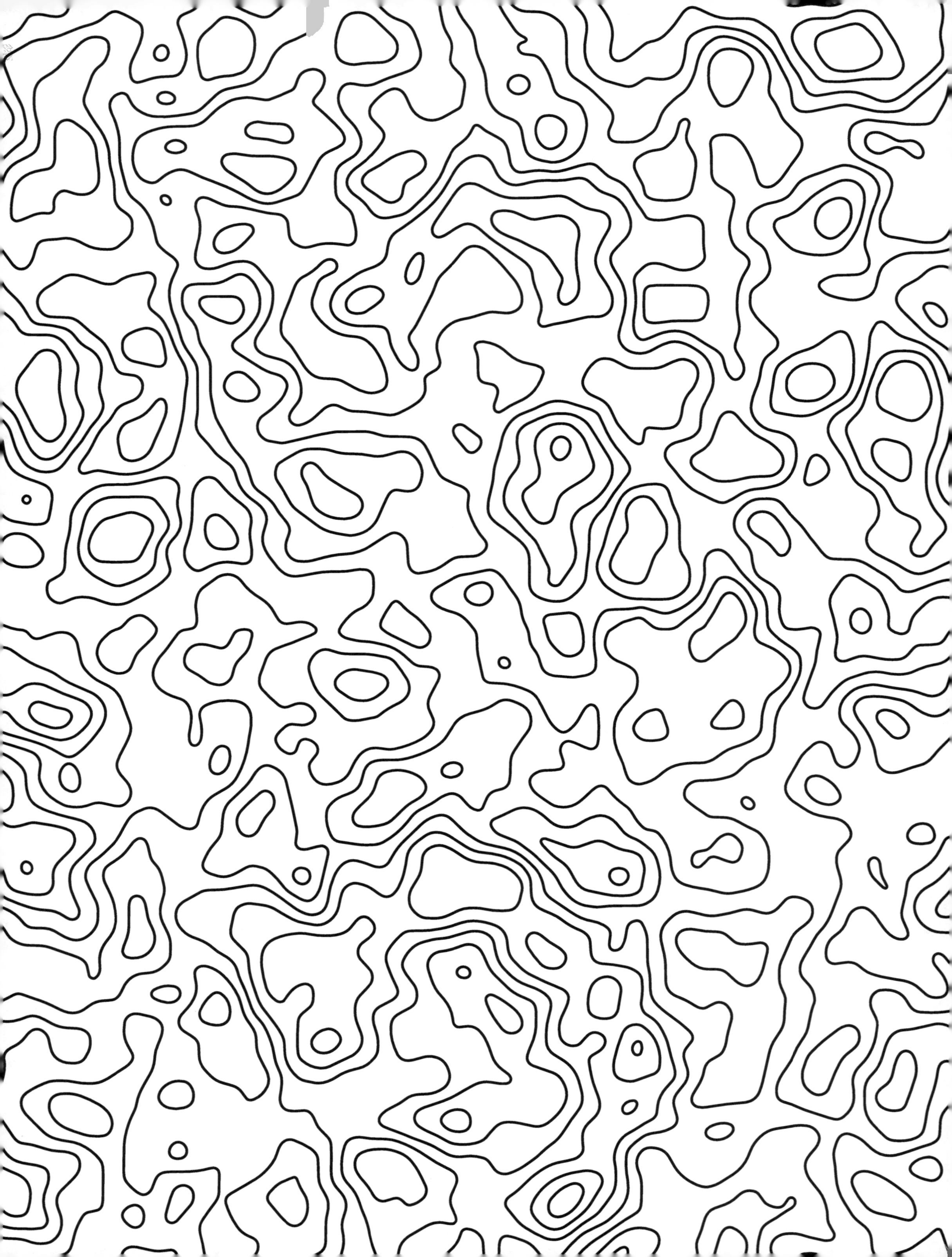

B
BUTTERFLY

Butterflies are very beautiful insects. They usually have bright colors like yellow, blue, and green.

Their bright colors help scare away predators.

B

Now, my little friend, let's try to write the letter 'B'.
Are you ready?

B B B _____

_____

_____

You've learned how to write the letter B. Great job!

But guess what? This butterfly needs your help! She got caught in the rain and lost all her colors. She's feeling sad and wants to be beautiful again.

Will you help her smile by coloring her?

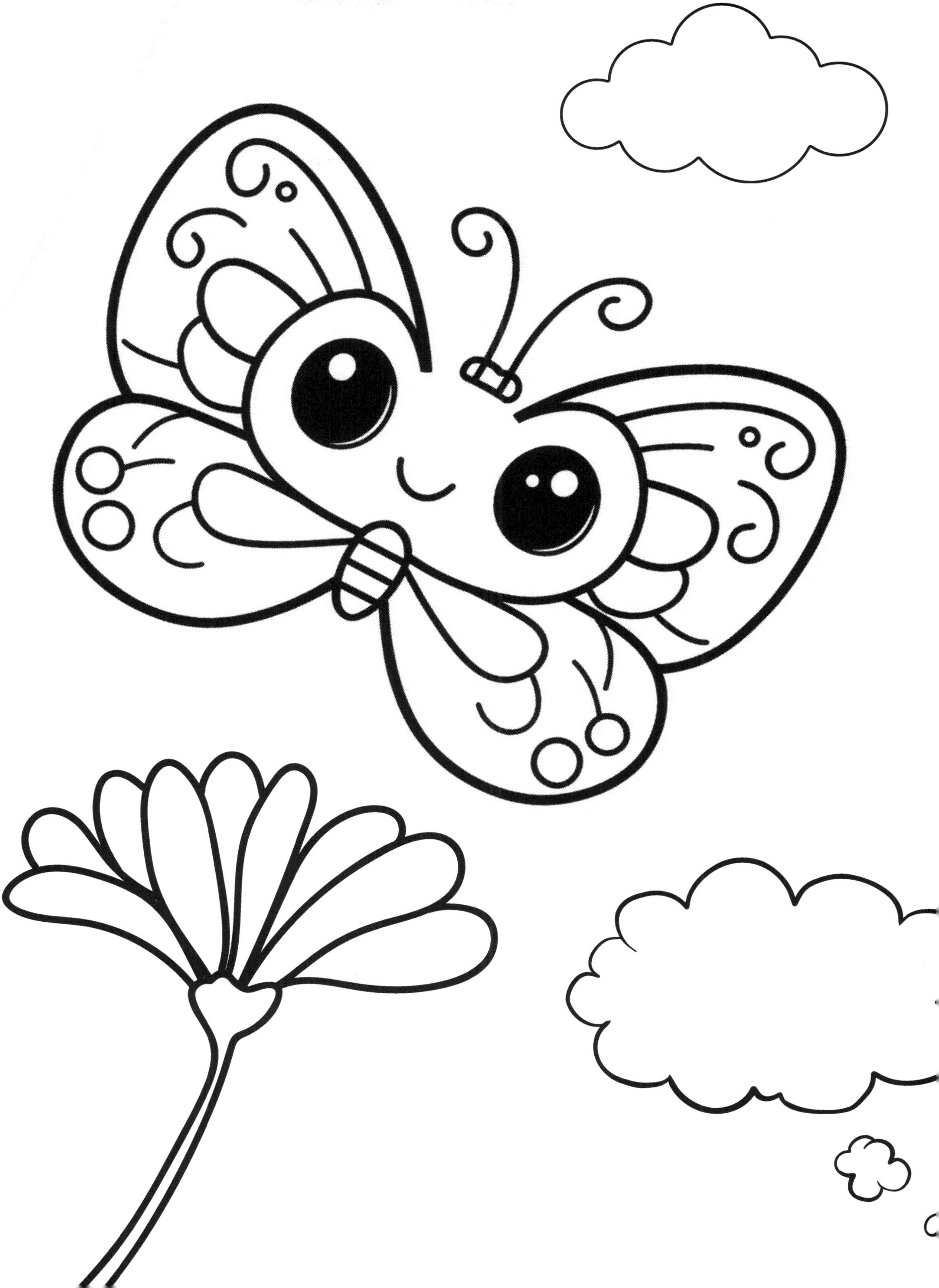

C CRAB

A crab is an animal that lives both in water and on land.

Crabs like to hide in shells to stay safe.

They help keep the water clean, which makes them very important.

C

Alright, my little friend, let's give writing the letter 'C' a try! Are you excited?

C C C _____

_____

_____

Well done my little friend! This crab has just returned from a long journey across the sea. He visited all the beaches, but there's a problem — his colors washed away! The crab really wants to be bright again.

Will you help him get his colors back?

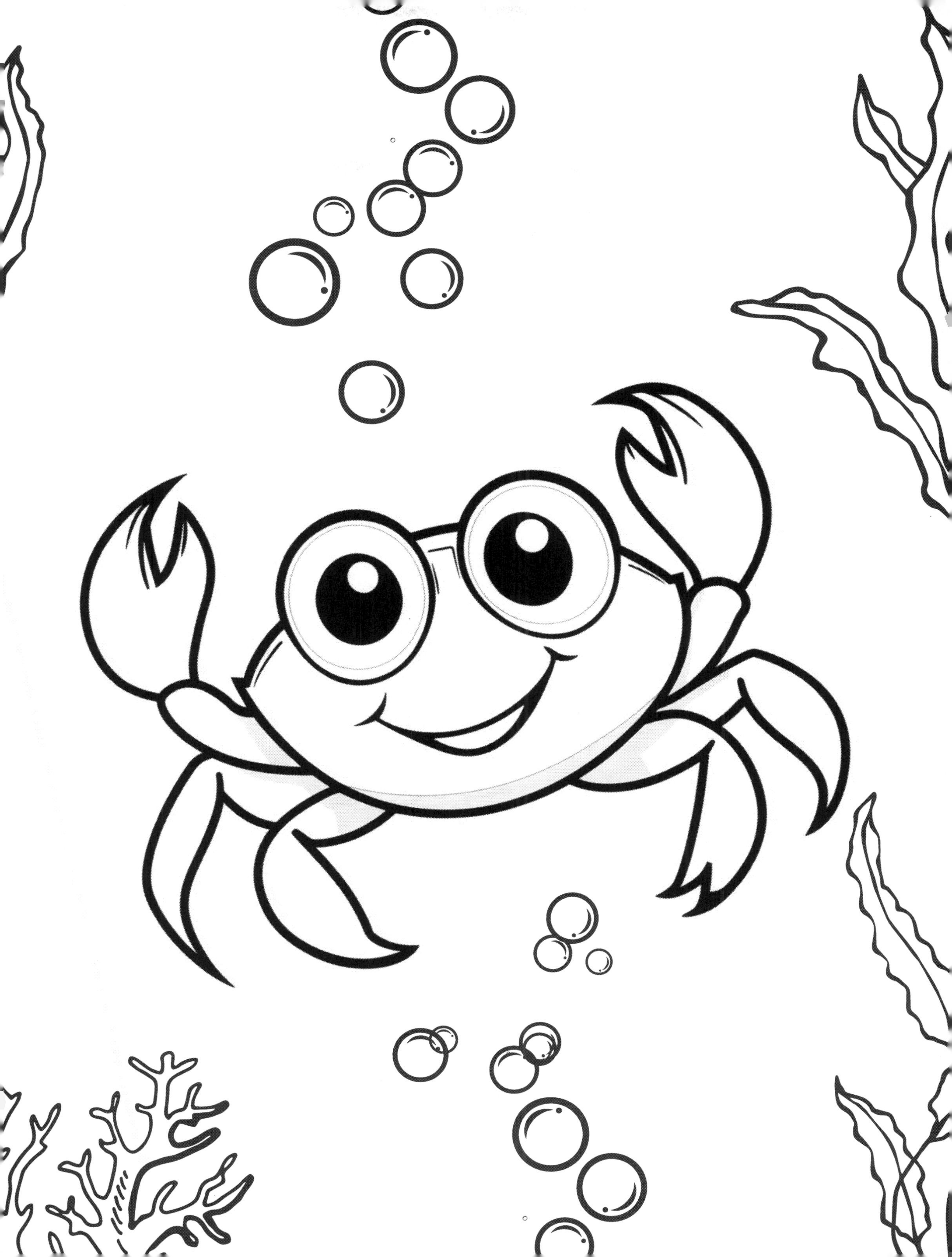

D DOLPHIN

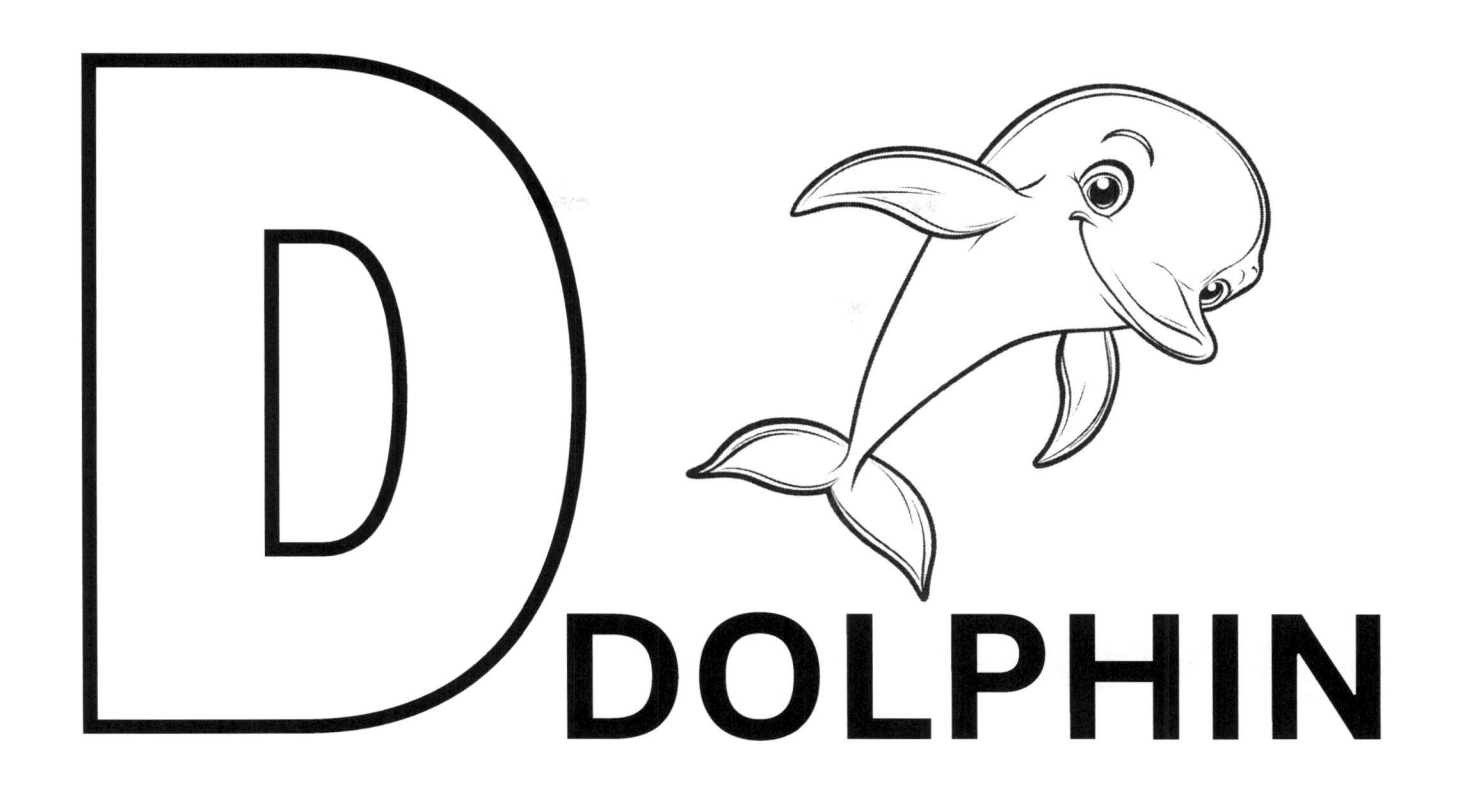

Dolphins are animals that live in the water.

They are very smart and love to play, often jumping out of the water.

Dolphins talk to each other using special sounds.

D

Okay, my little friend, let's give writing the letter 'D' a try!

Are you ready to begin?

D D D _____

_____

_____

This dolphin really wants to be your friend, but he's shy because he lost his bright colors.

If you color him, he will happily become your friend.

Will you help him?

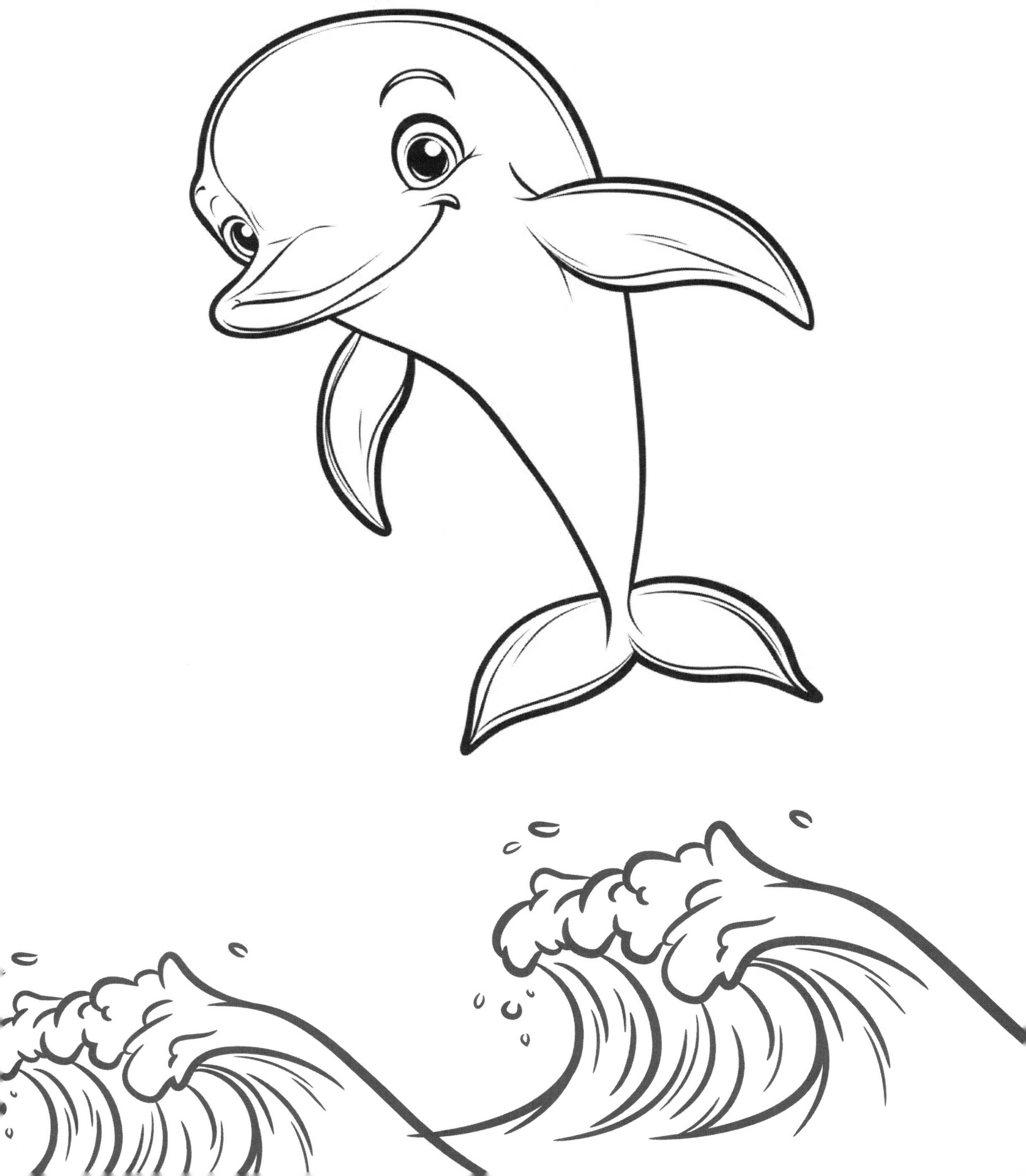

E

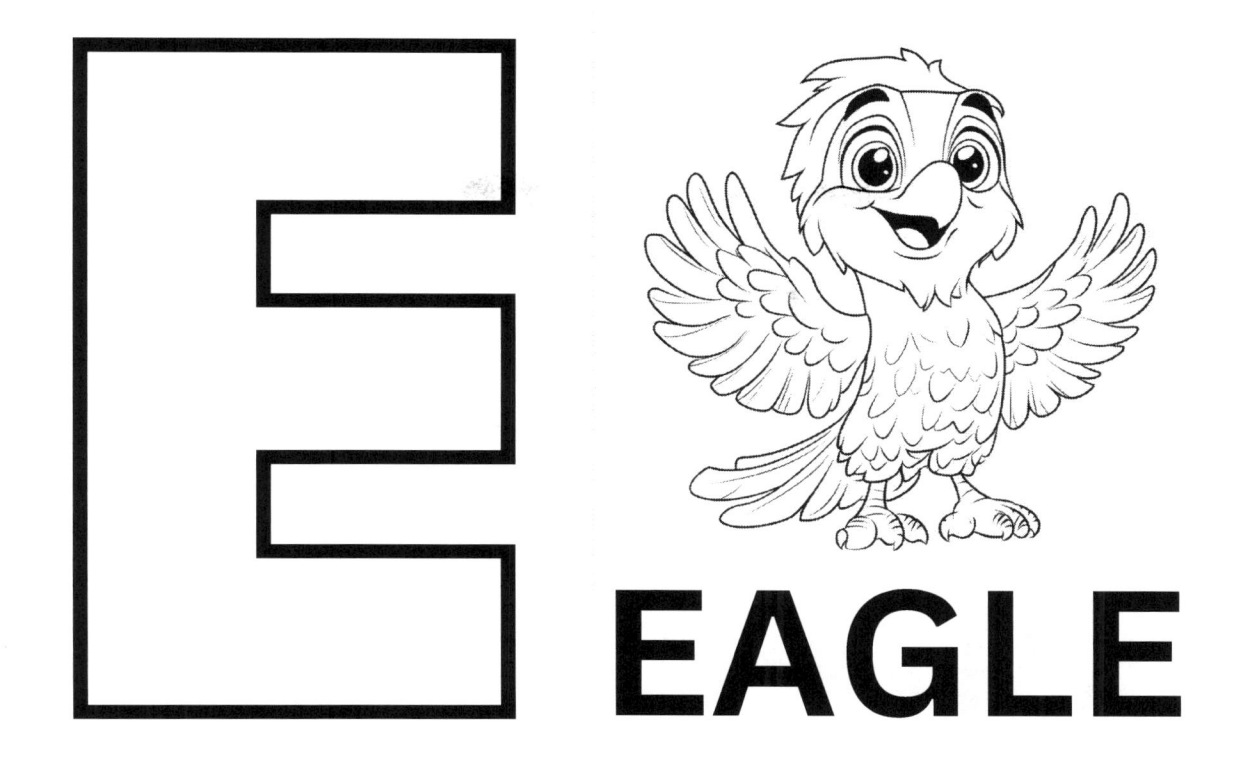

EAGLE

Eagles are large birds that are called the kings of the sky! They are smart and have excellent vision. Eagles can fly high and soar in the sky for a long time.

They build their nests on tall trees or cliffs and catch their prey with sharp claws. They live in nests on tall trees or cliffs.

E

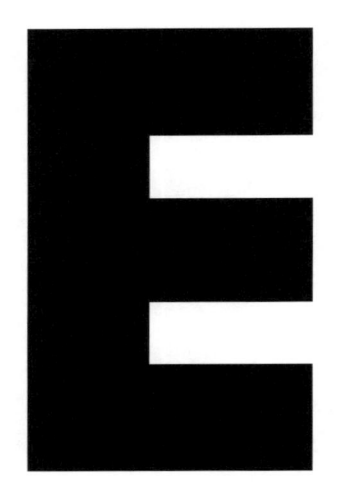

Now, my little friend, let's try to write the letter 'E'.

Are you ready?

E E E _____

_____

_____

This eagle has come to you for help. He wants you to think of what colors he could be and to color him in.

Will you help him choose some good colors?

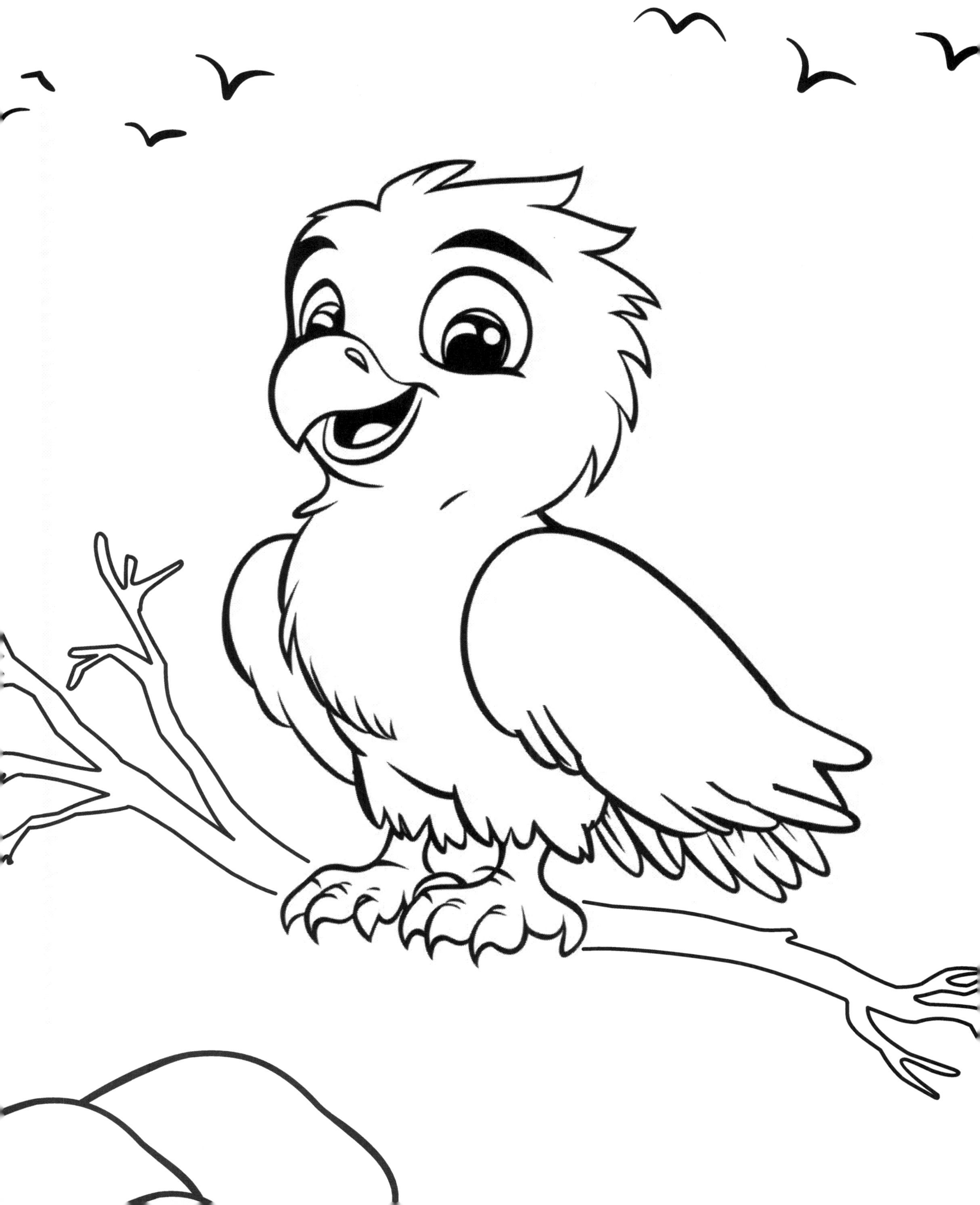

F FOX

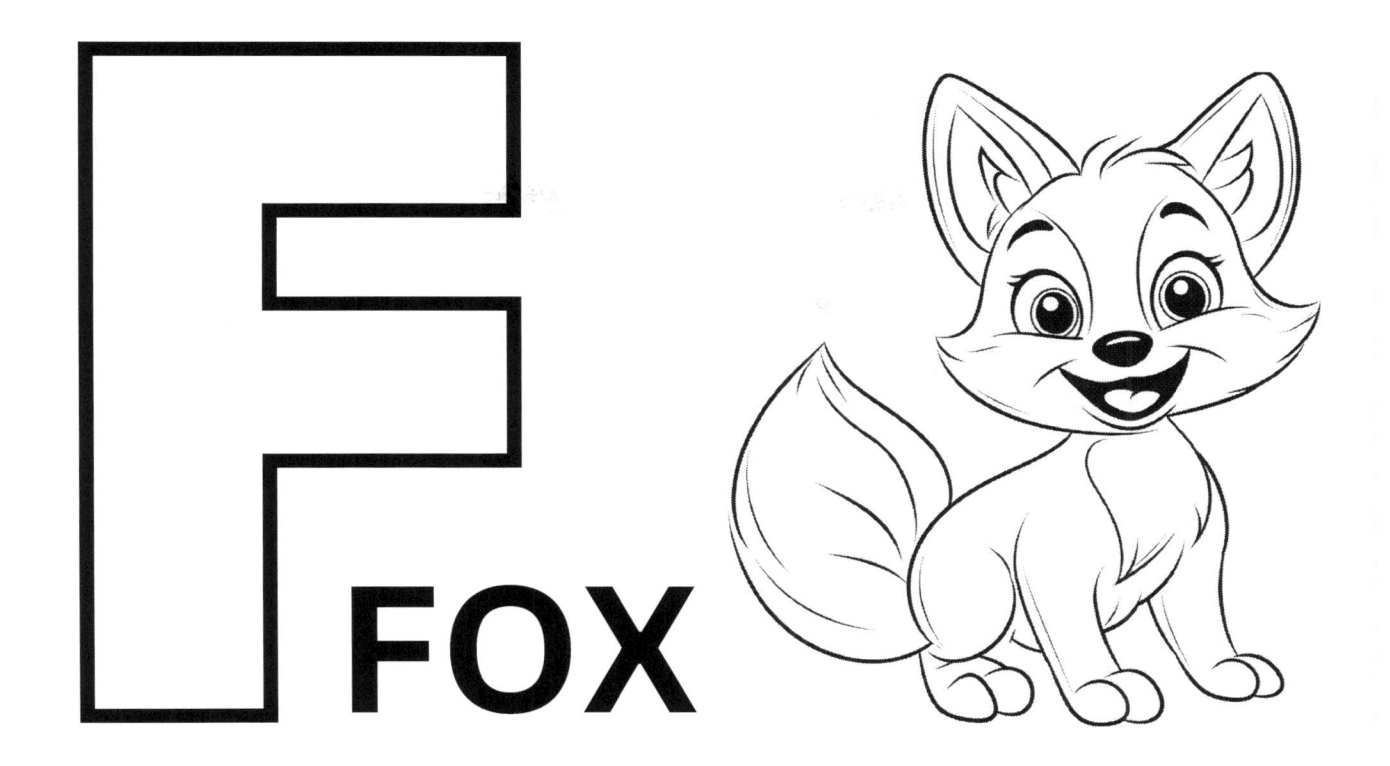

Foxes are clever creatures of the forest.

They live in burrows that they dig themselves.

Their fluffy tails and reddish fur make them very beautiful.

F

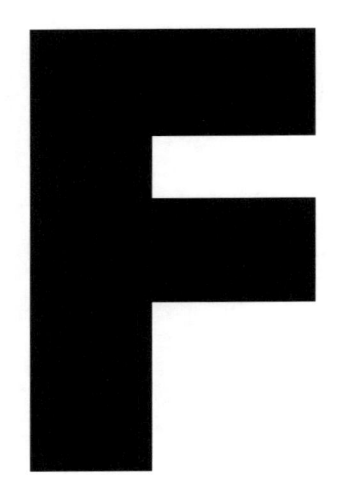

Now, my little friend, let's try to write the letter 'F'. Are you ready?

F F F _____

_____

_____

The eagle told this fox that you did a great job coloring him, and now she wants to be colorful too!

Will you help her?

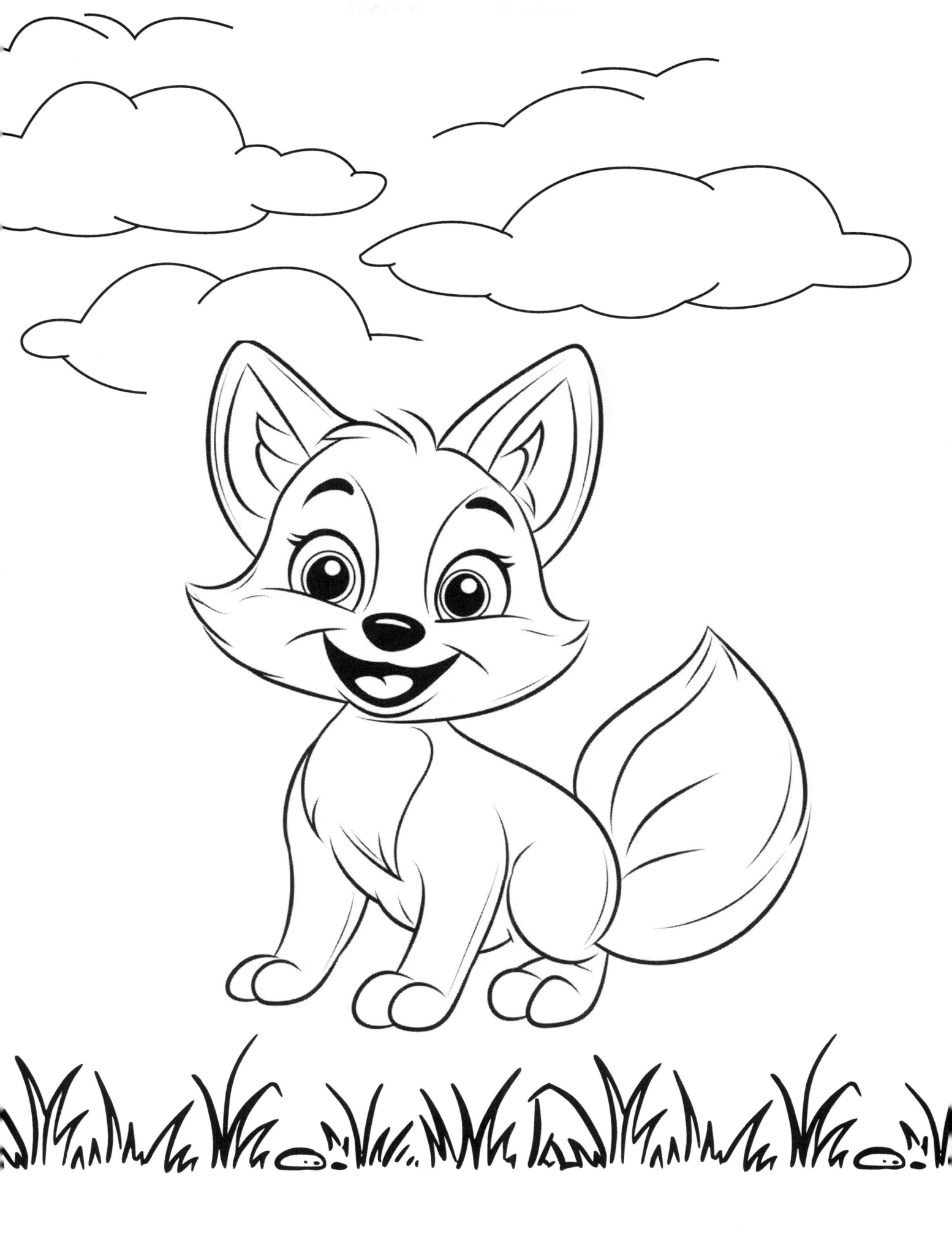

G GECKO

Geckos are little lizards, but some can grow really long—up to 23 inches. That's as long as a big ruler!

They have sticky feet that help them climb walls and even ceilings.

If a gecko is in danger, it may shed its tail, especially if attacked. But don't worry, the tail will grow back.

G

Alright, my little friend, let's give writing the letter 'G' a try!
Are you excited?

G G G
_____

_____

_____

Geckos can be all sorts of different colors! This gecko has decided he wants to be unique.

What color do you think would be best to color him?

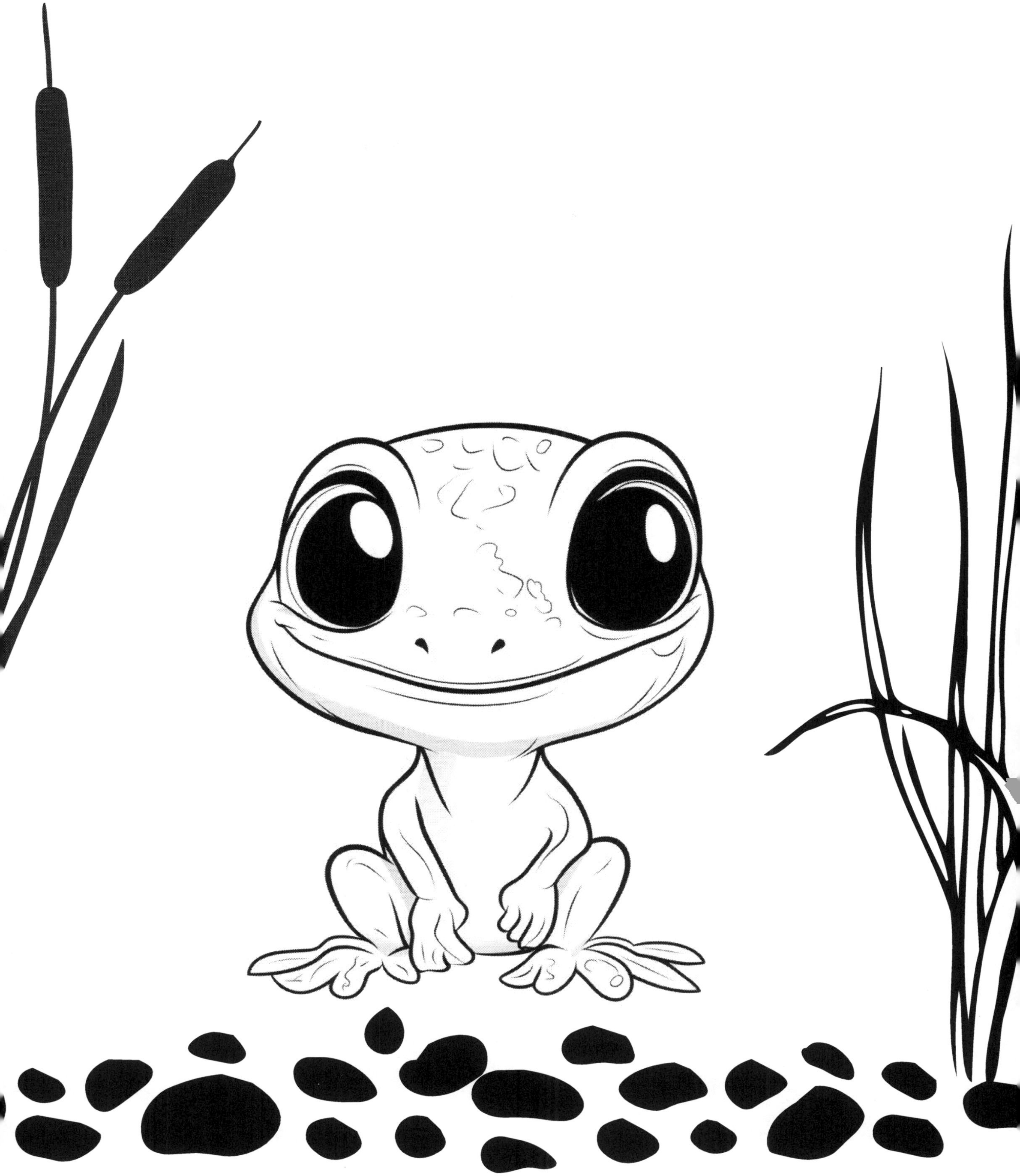

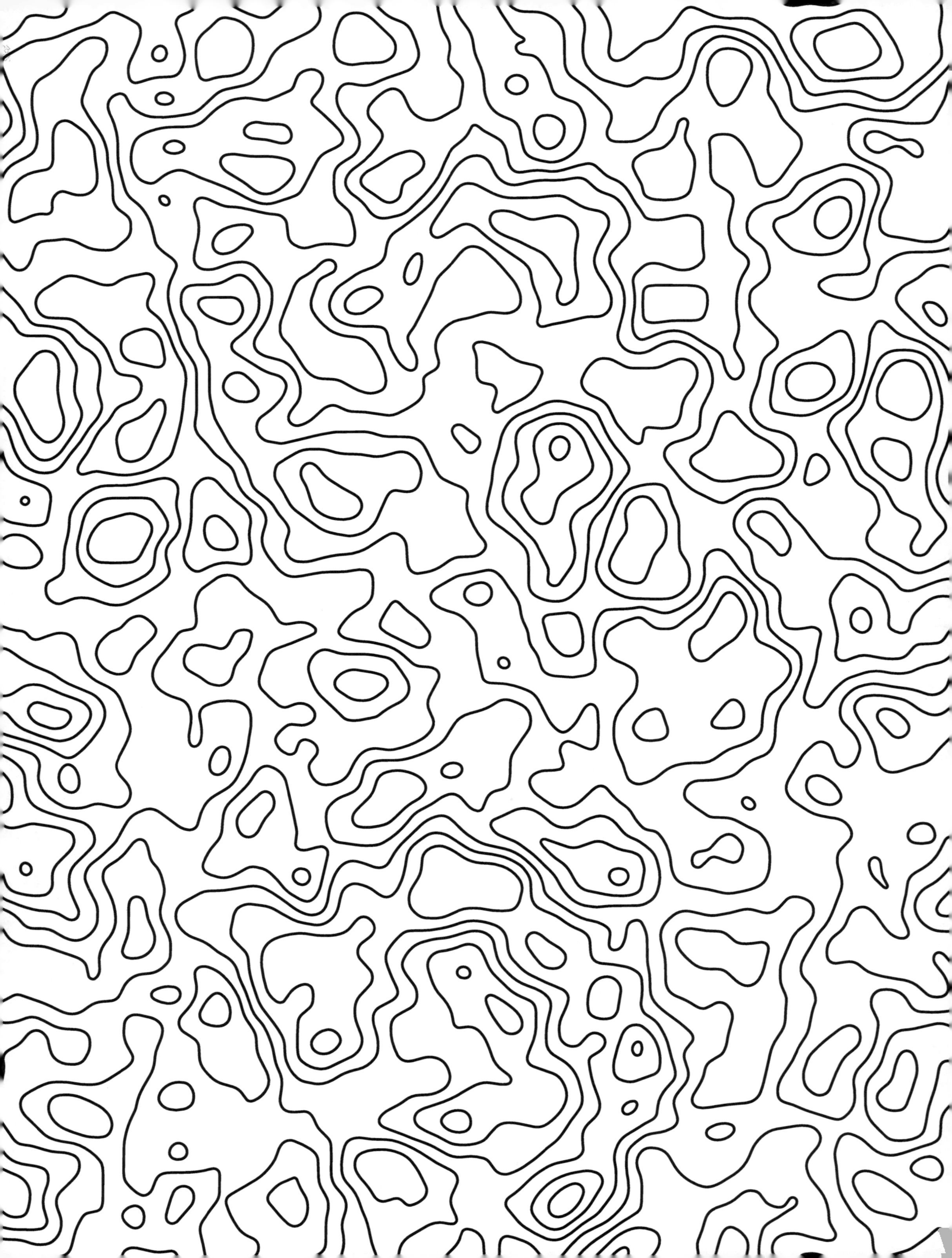

H
HEDGEHOG

A hedgehog is a forest animal. Almost all of its body is covered in spines. An adult hedgehog can have between 5,000 and 7,000 spines.

When in danger, the hedgehog curls up into a spiky ball, and no predator can harm him.

H

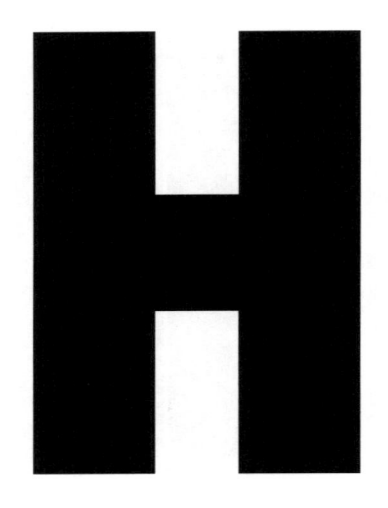

Okay, my little friend, let's practice writing the letter 'H' together! Ready to start?

H H H

This hedgehog is very scared. He was also caught in the magical rain. And now he needs your help!

Can you help him and color him in?

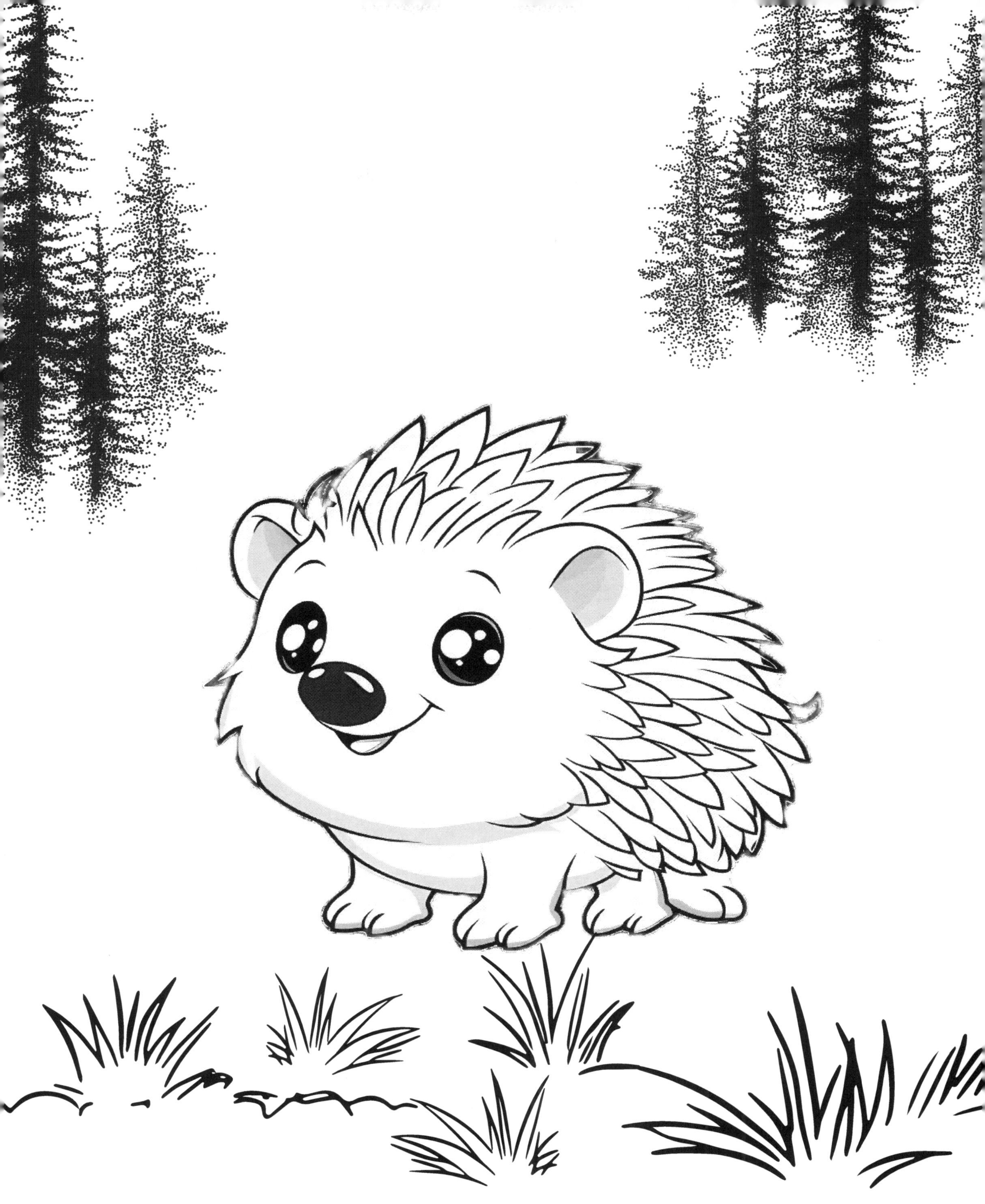

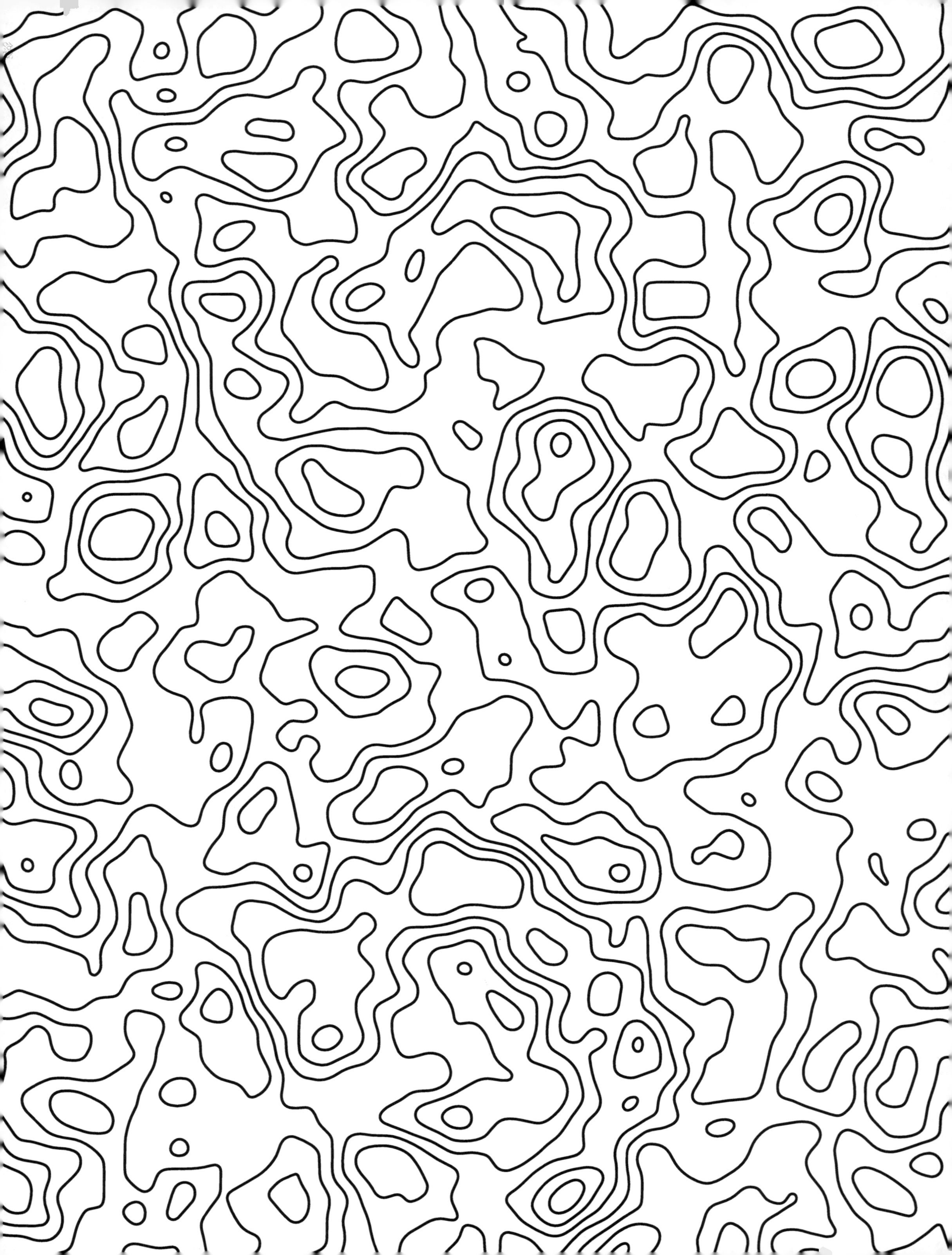

I IGUANA

Iguanas are cool green lizards that love to climb trees and soak up the sun!
They eat plants like leaves and fruits, making them big salad fans. Iguanas have long tails to help them swim and balance, and their eyes can see all around.
These super swimmers and sun-lovers are full of fun surprises. Sometimes iguanas move their tails or heads to greet each other.

I

Now, my little friend, let's try to write the letter 'I'. Are you ready?

| | |

An iguana knocked on your door. Look at him, he is so unhappy. It used to be so bright and proud of its colors, but the magical rain took them away. The Iguana really needs your help!

Can you color him?

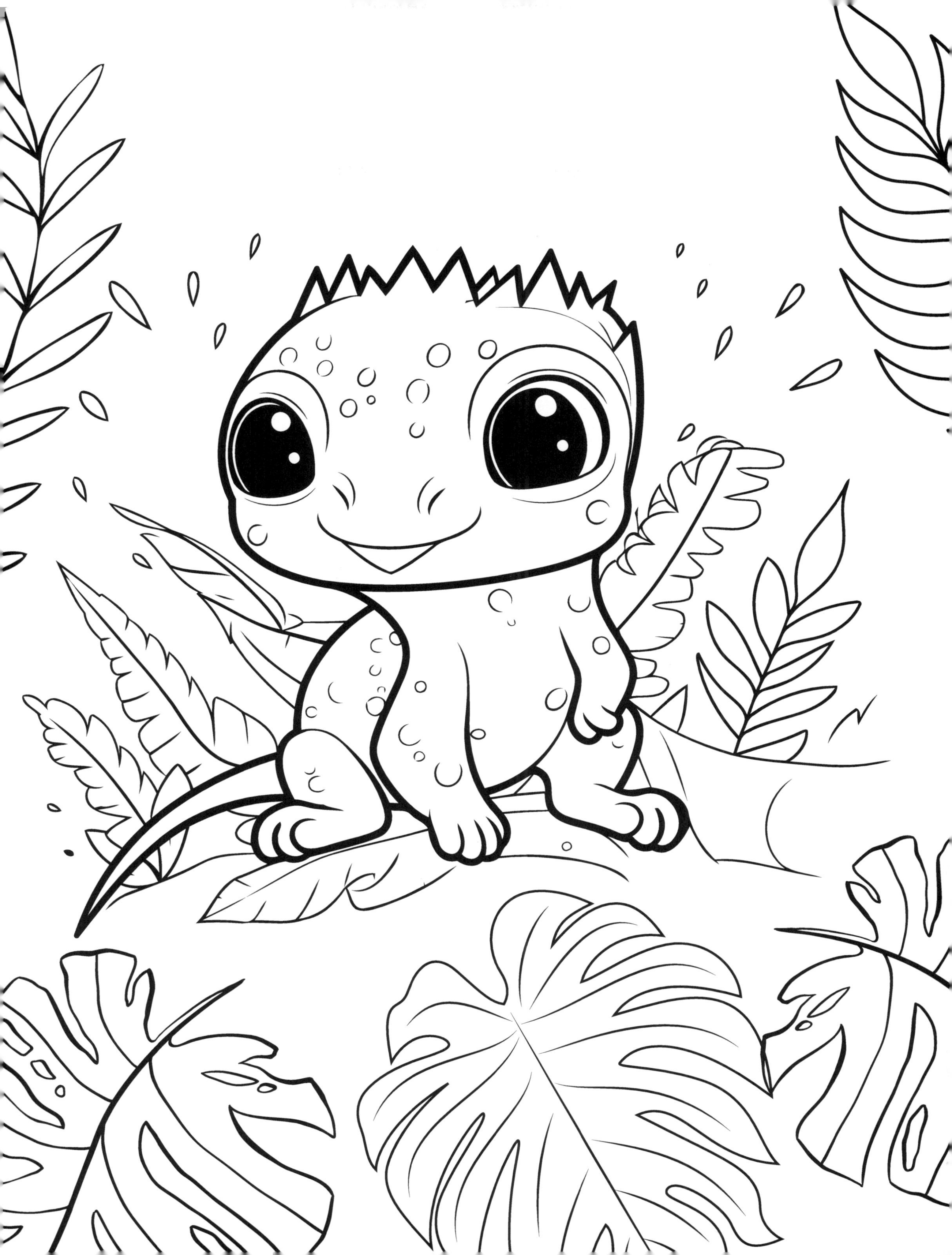

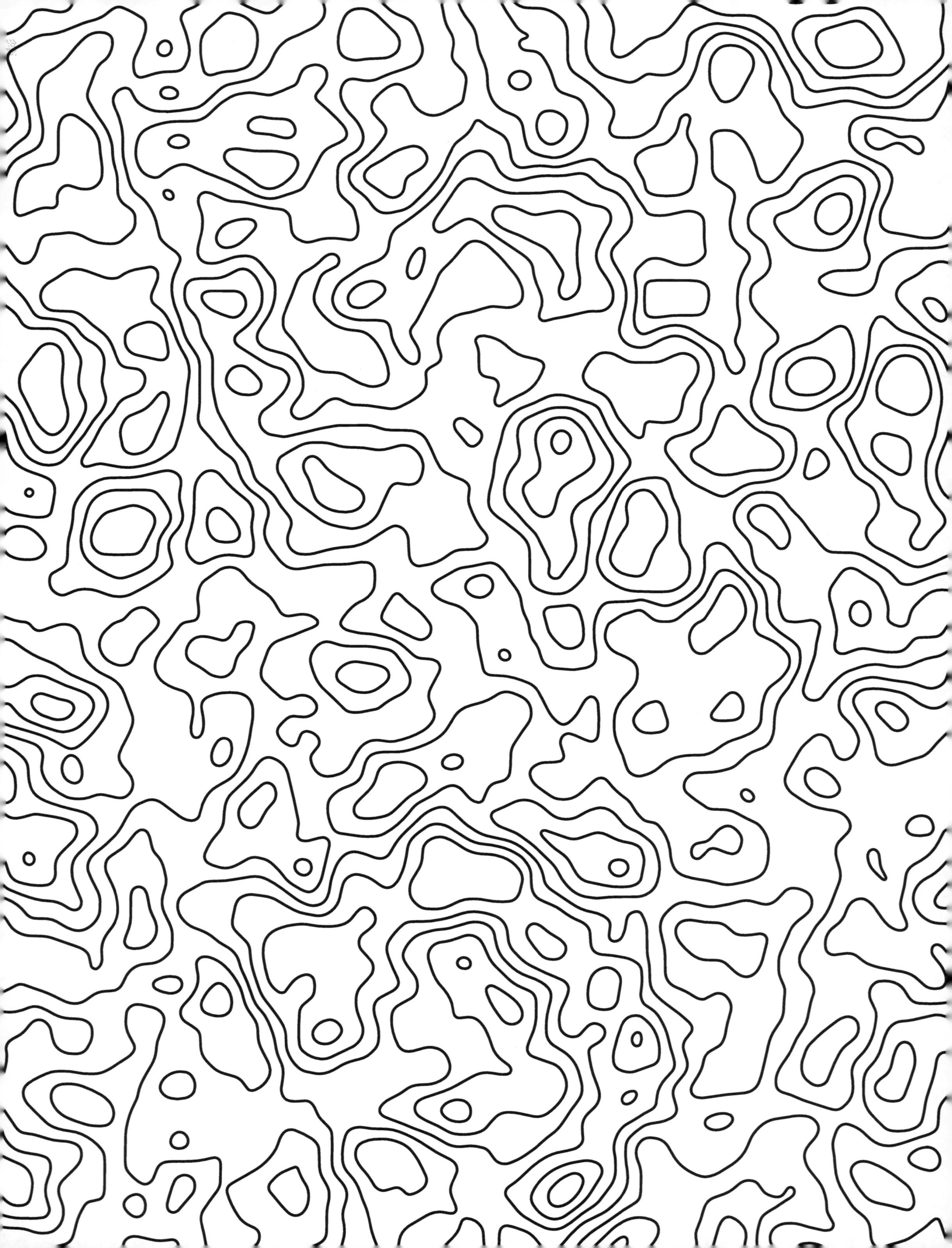

J JAGUAR

Jaguars are big jungle cats. Unlike house cats, they are great swimmers! Jaguars are famous for their strength and hunting skills.

Jaguars have golden fur with black spots shaped like roses. Each jaguar has a unique pattern of spots, just like humans have unique fingerprints!

J

**Now, my little friend, let's try to write the letter 'J'.
Are you ready?**

J J J

This little jaguar has come to you for bright colors.

Use your magic pencils and markers to color him!

Let the jaguar feel happy!

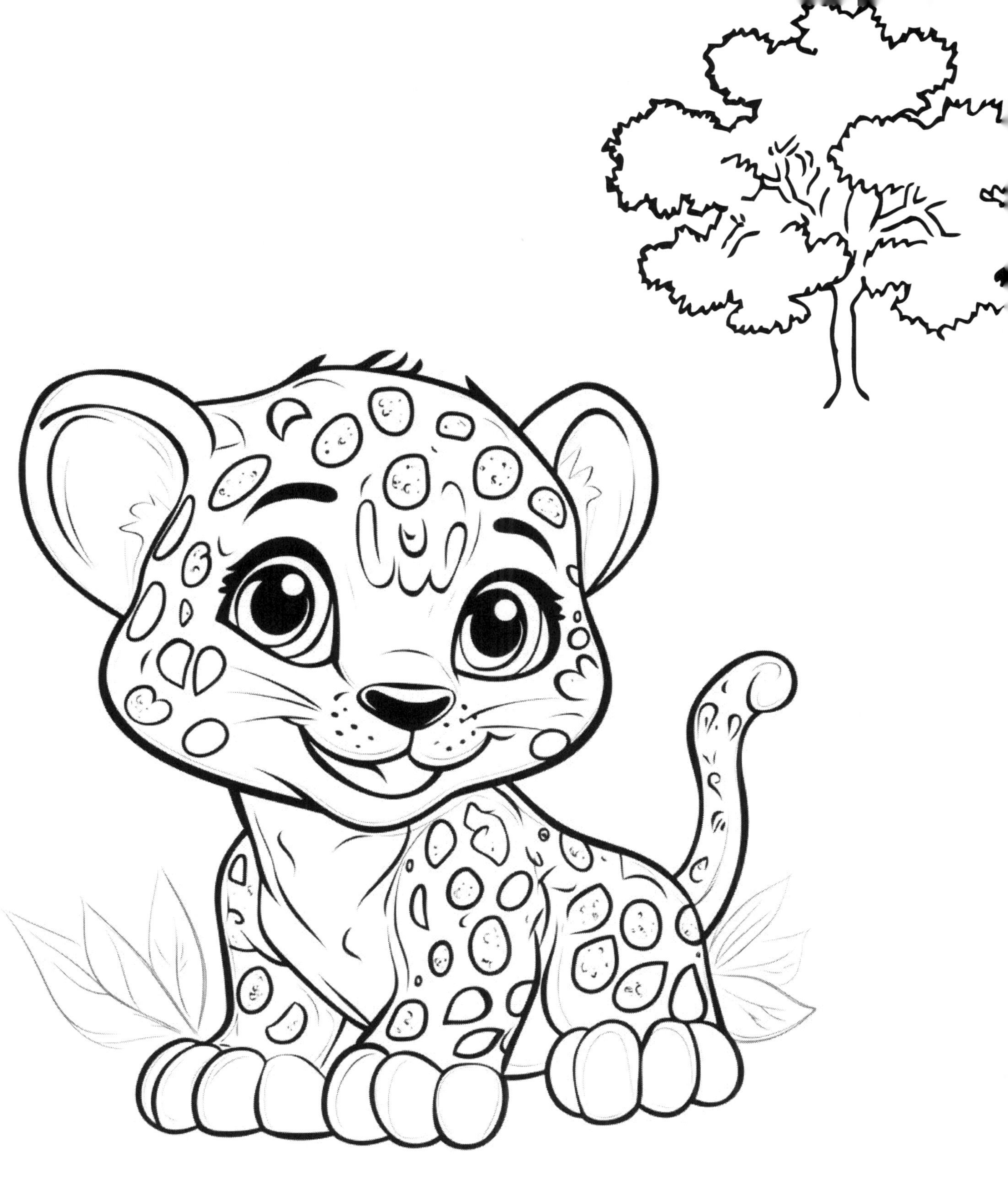

KANGAROO

Kangaroos are amazing animals; they are super strong and full of surprises. They don't walk like we do—they hop! Their powerful legs help them jump really far, sometimes as far as a whole car.

Kangaroos have a special pouch on their tummy where they carry their baby, called a joey, to keep it safe and warm. Isn't that cool?

Did you know kangaroos can't walk backward? They can only move forward!

K

*Okay, my little friend, let's practice writing the letter 'K' together!
Ready to start?*

K K K _____

_____

_____

This black and white kangaroo recently got a visit from his friend, the hedgehog.

The hedgehog told the kangaroo how great you are at coloring, and now the kangaroo wants to be colorful too.

Are you ready to color the mother kangaroo and her baby?

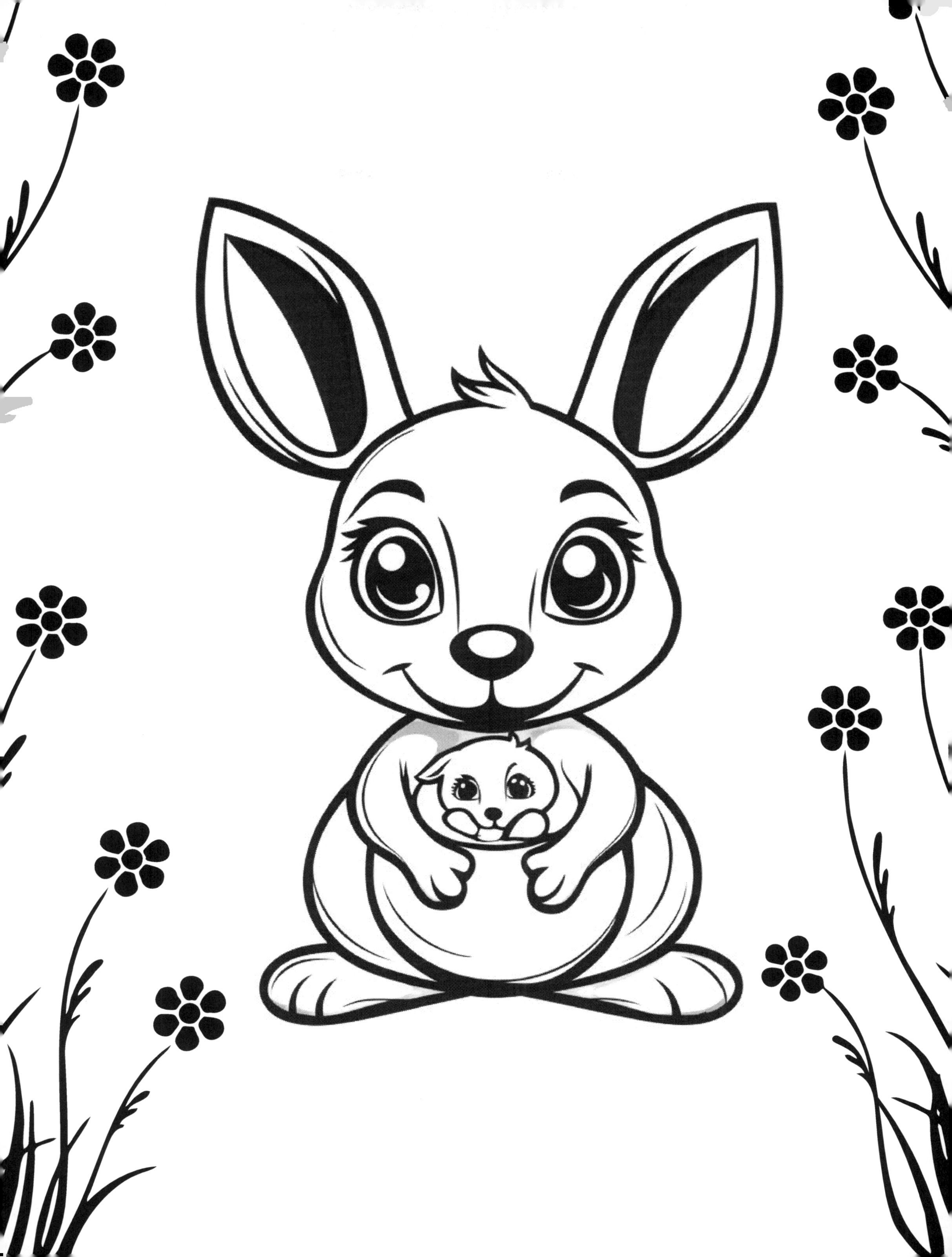

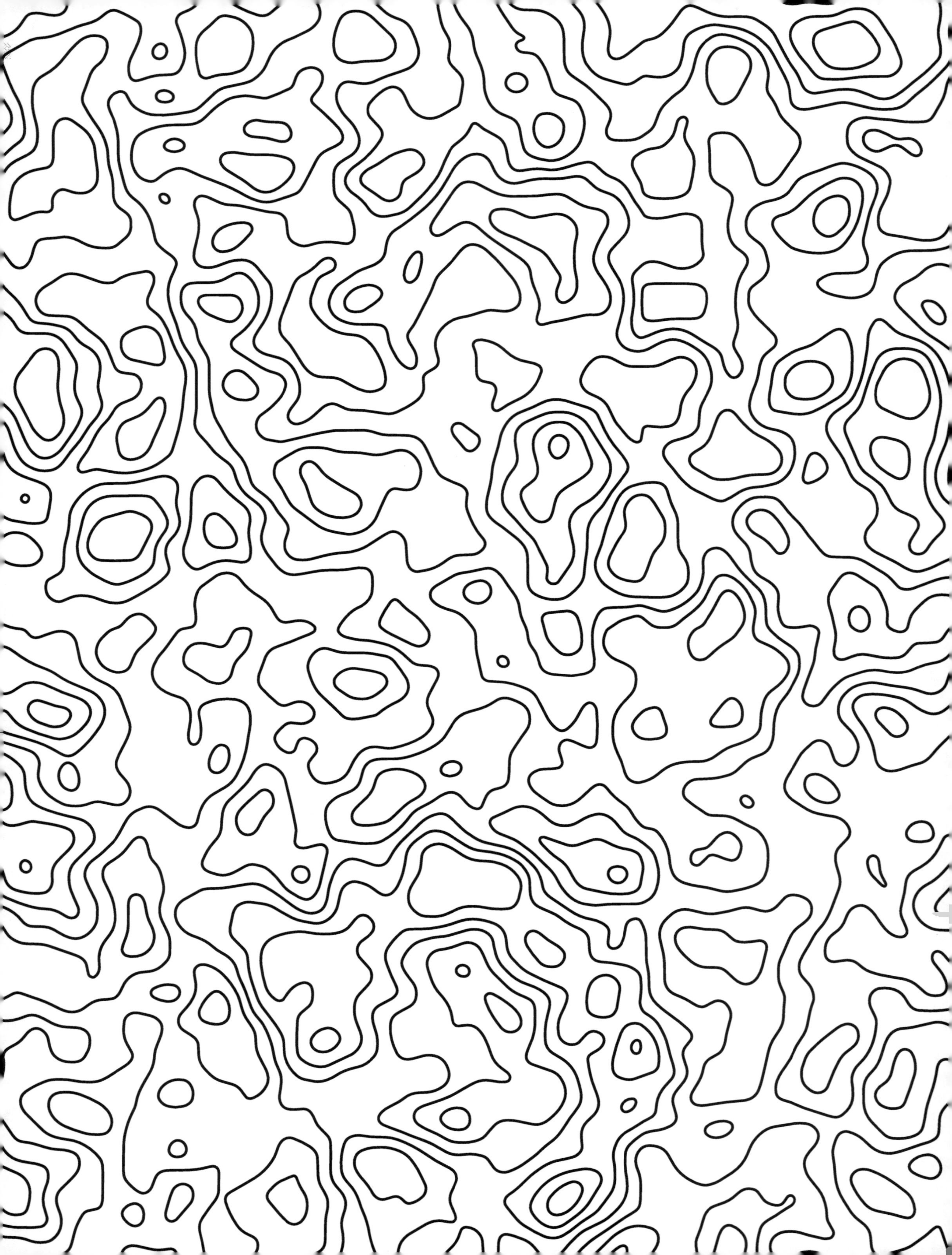

L LADYBUG

Ladybugs are tiny, helpful insects that love to eat small bugs called aphids, which harm plants. This makes ladybugs great friends for gardens!

Ladybugs can also fly! They have wings tucked under their hard, colorful shells.

Because of their bright colors and helpful nature, ladybugs are considered symbols of luck and happiness in many cultures around the world.

L

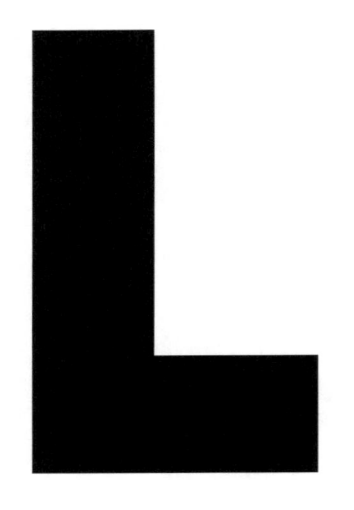

Now, my little friend, let's try to write the letter 'L'. Are you ready?

L L L

This ladybug has lost not only her colors but also her spots. Without her bright colors, she can't protect herself from predators, and without her spots, she can't bring good luck.

Will you help her regain her magical powers?

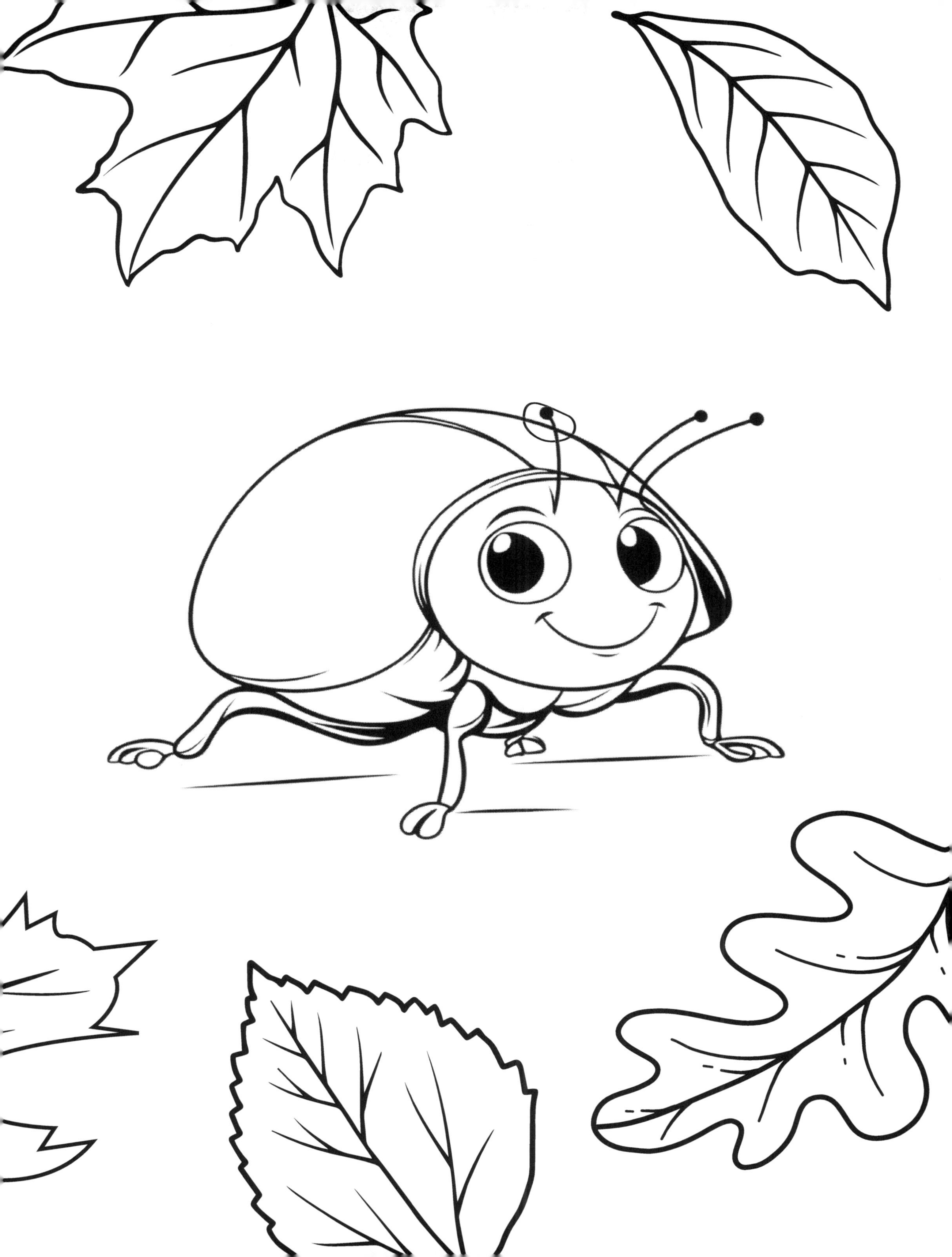

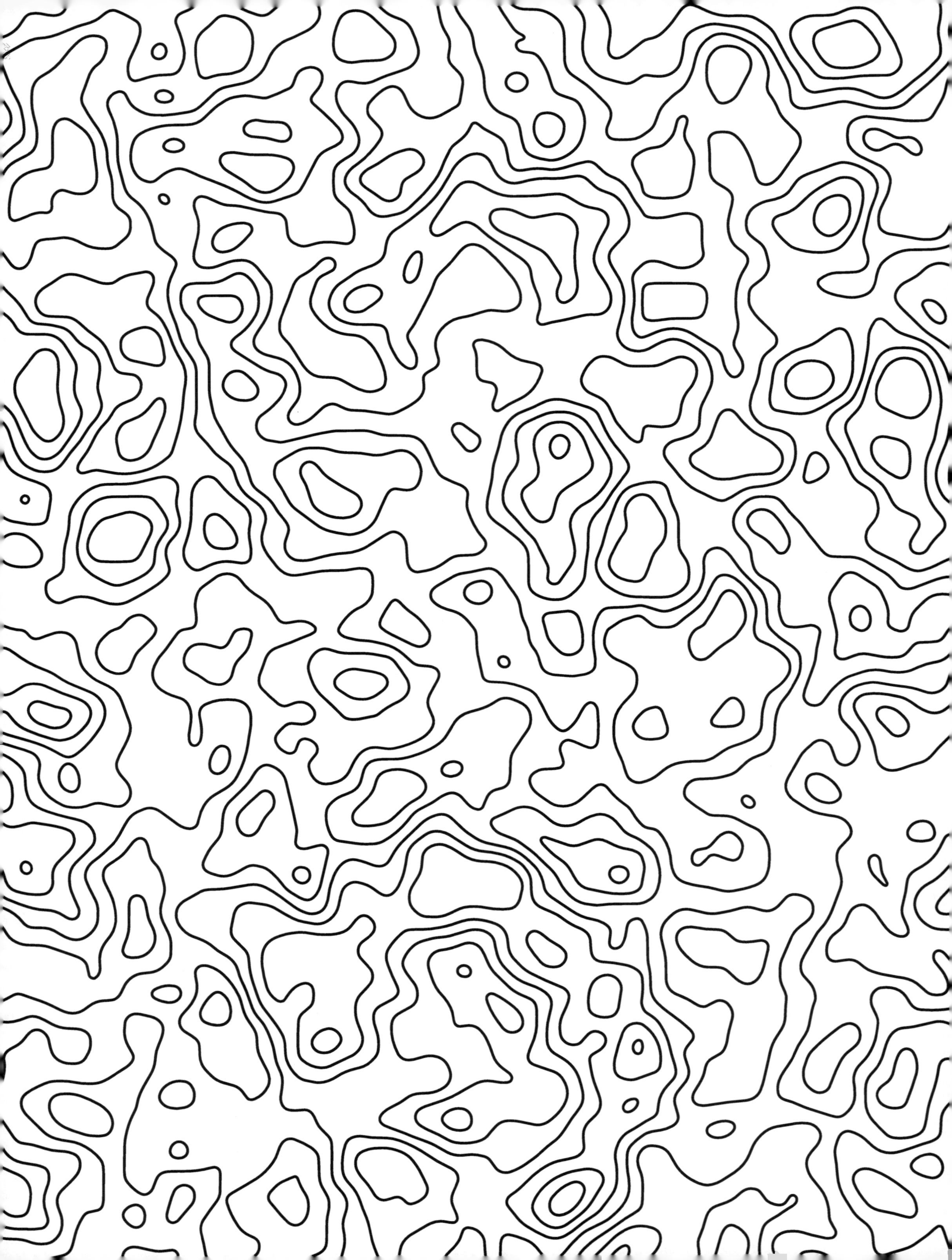

M MOOSE

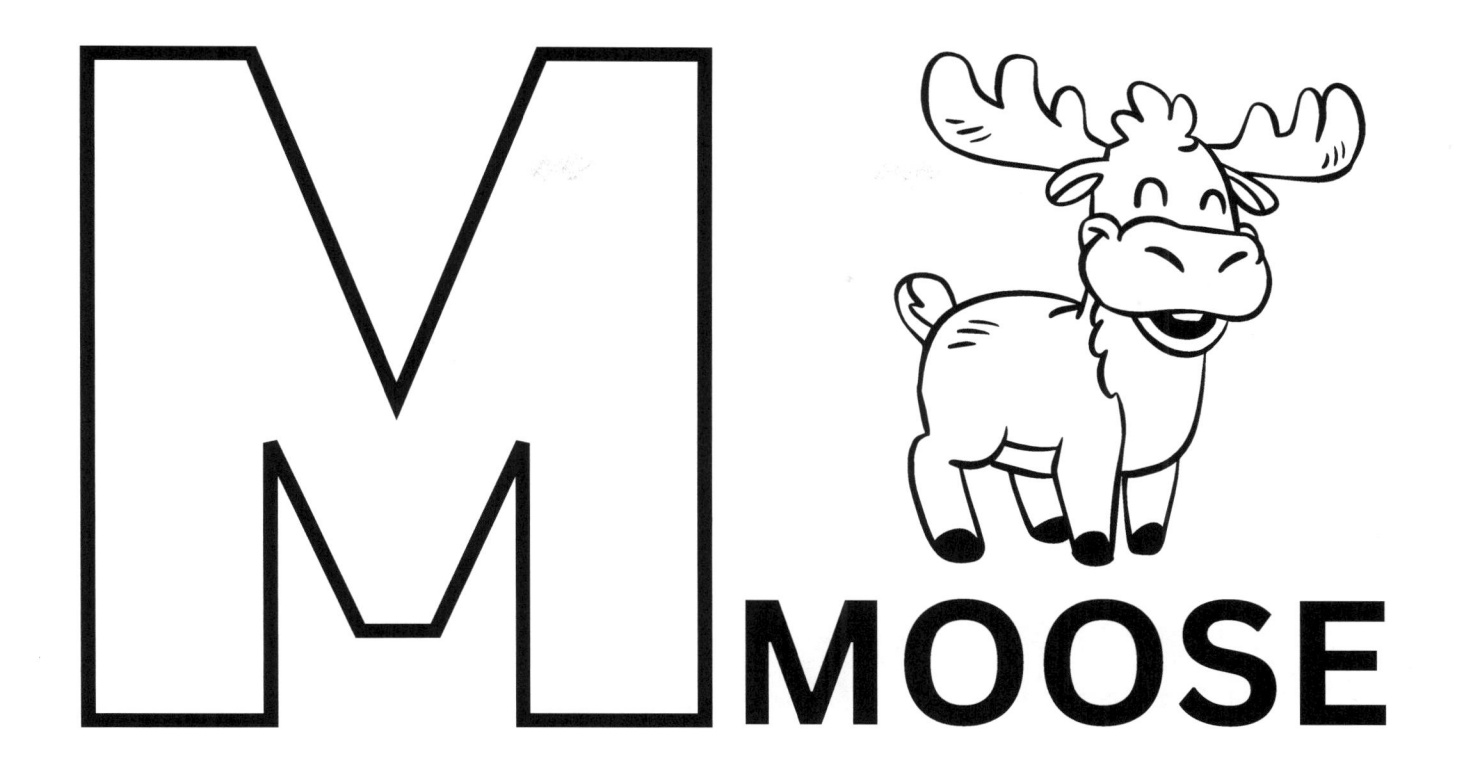

Moose are big animals, as tall as a grown-up! They have huge, branched antlers that can be very heavy—almost like carrying a big bag of toys!

They are excellent swimmers and can travel long distances across rivers and lakes. They also can hold their breath underwater to eat plants!

M

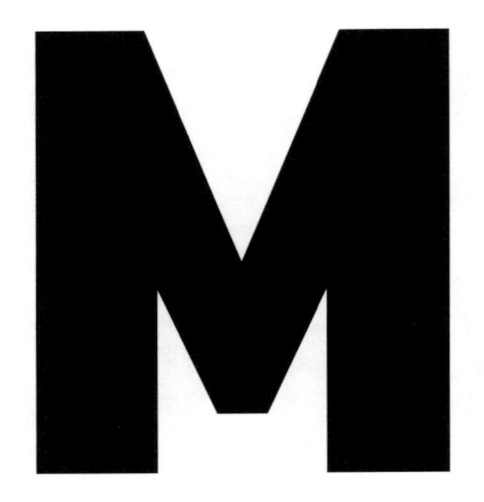

Alright, my little friend, let's give writing the letter 'M' a try!
Are you excited?

M M M
_____

_____

_____

This time, a majestic moose with large antlers has appeared on your doorstep. He looks a bit sad because he's lost his colors.

Will you help him become magnificent and beautiful again?

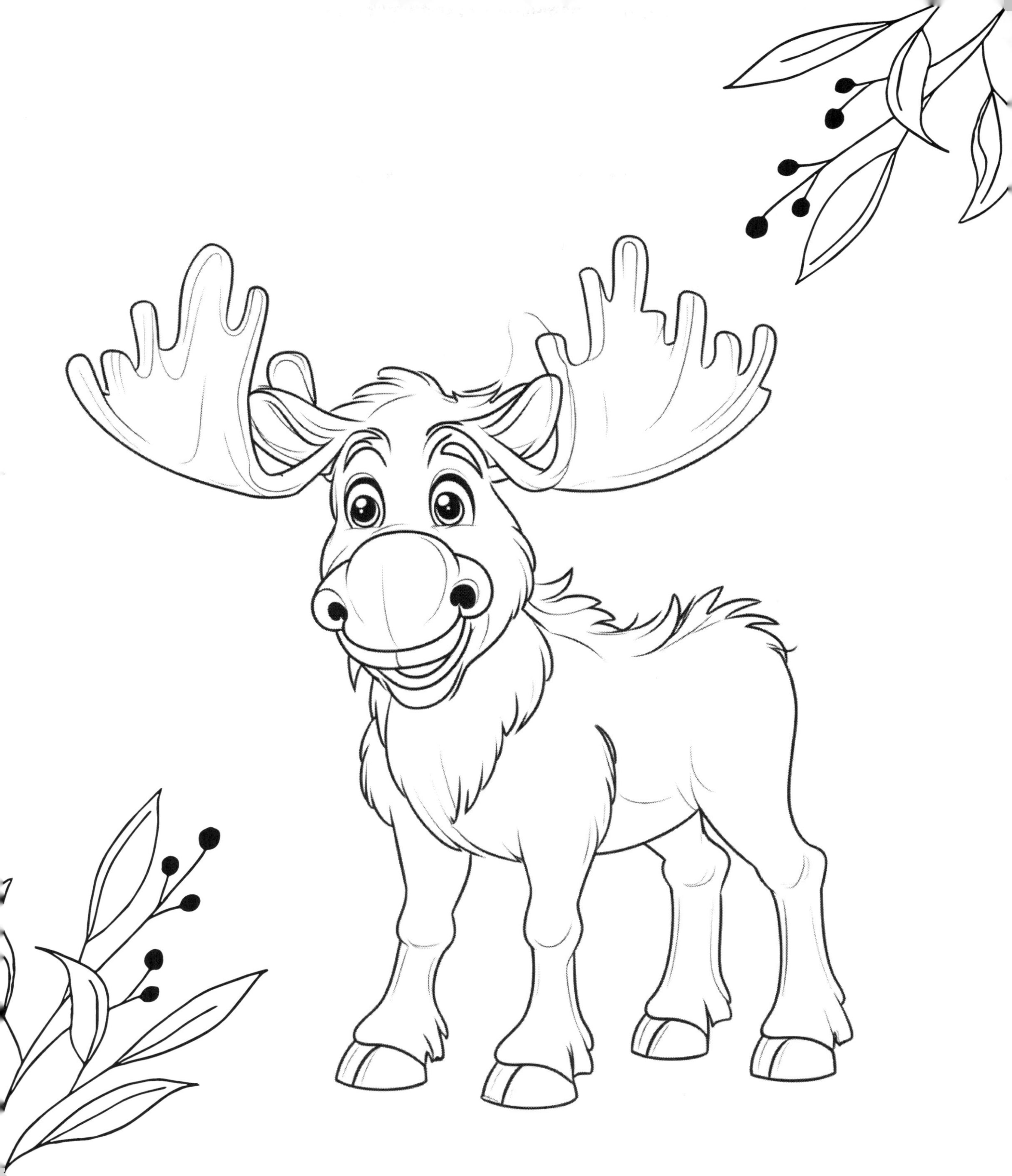

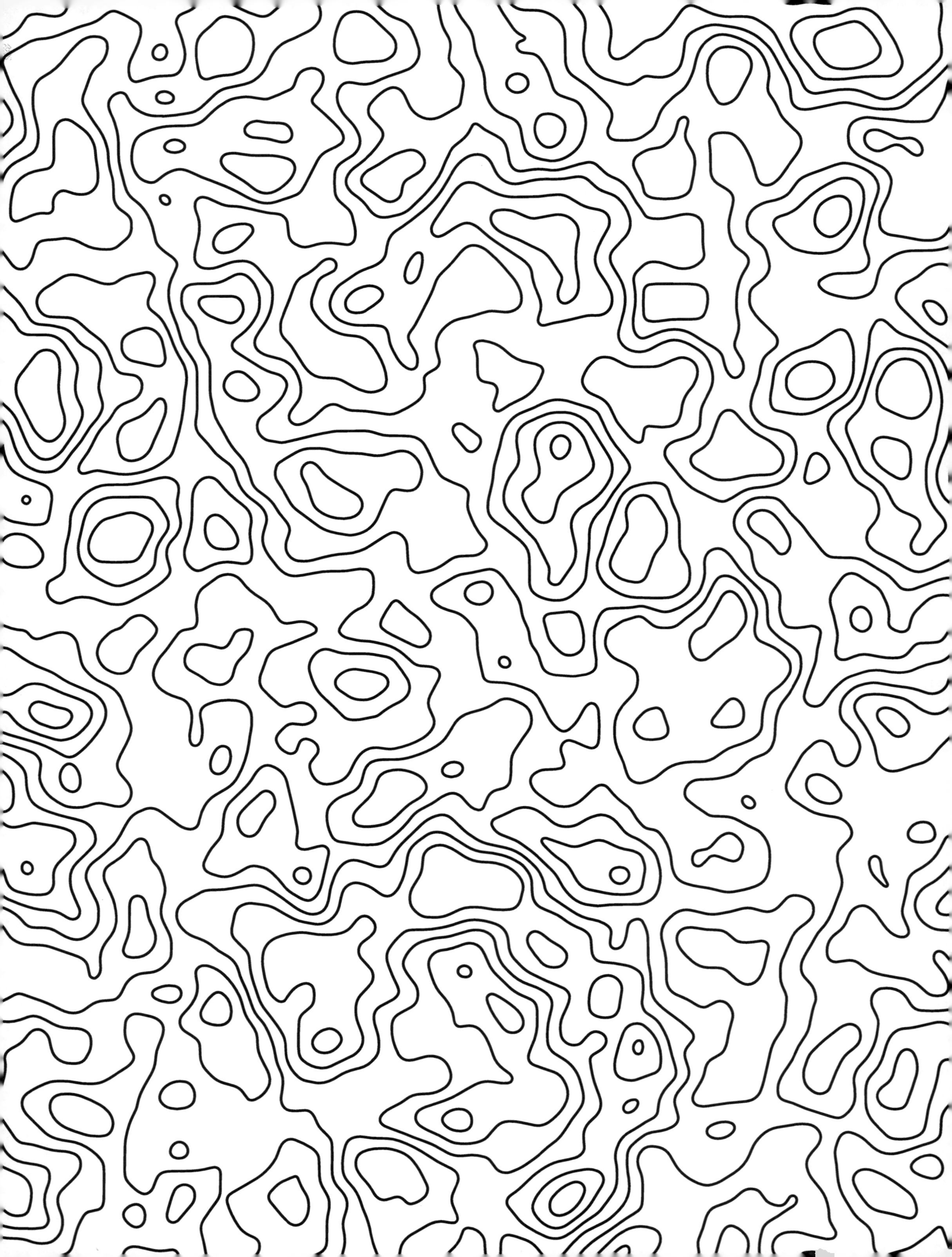

N NARVAL

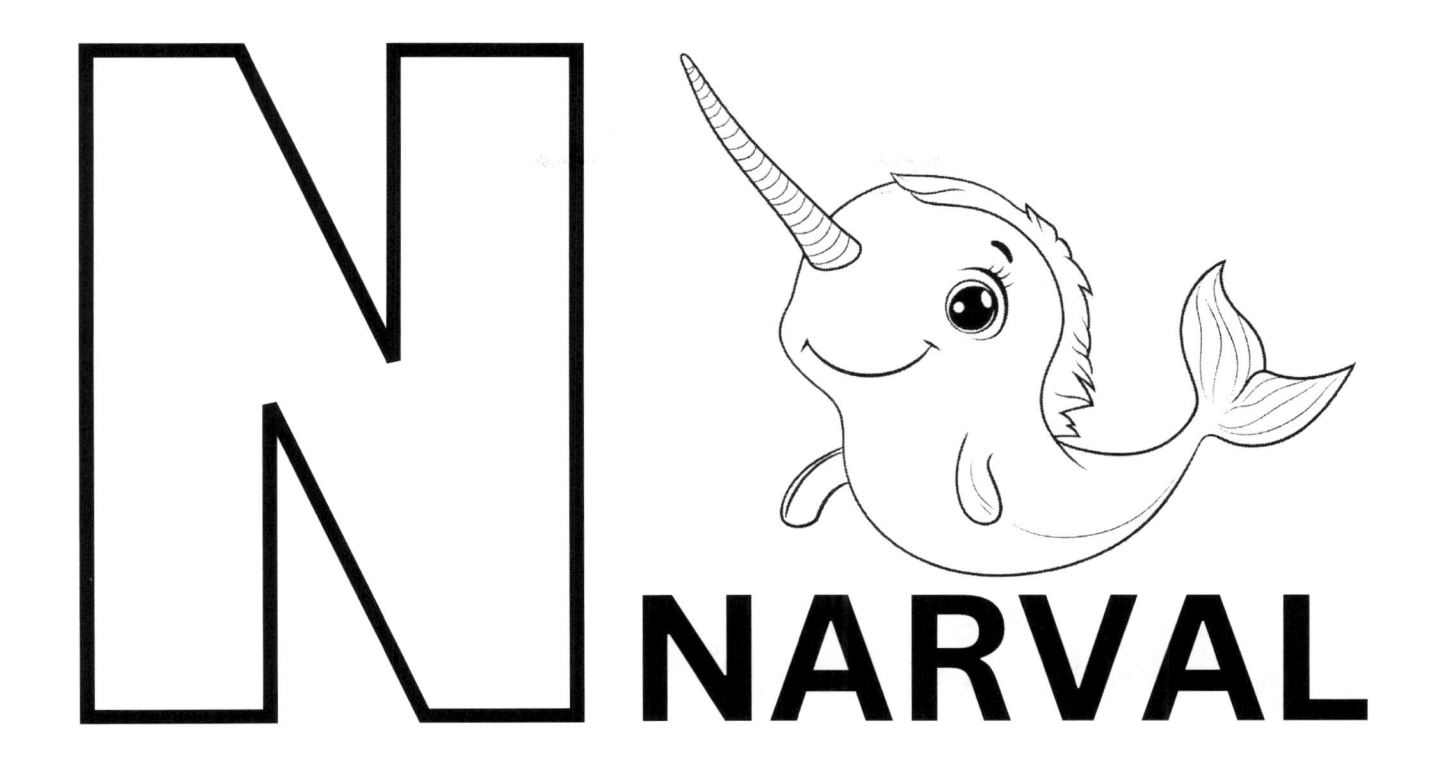

A narwhal is a unique sea creature, often called the 'unicorn of the sea' because of its long tusk that resembles a horn.

A narwhal has a long tusk that can grow as big as 10 feet—longer than a boat! They use their tusk to find food and to talk to their narwhal friends.

N

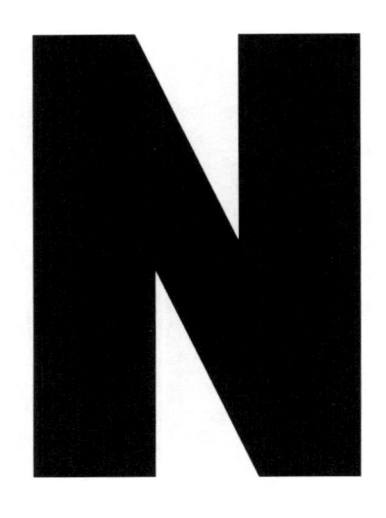

Okay, my little friend, let's practice writing the letter 'N' together! Ready to start?

N N N
_____

_____

_____

This narwhal heard that you have the power to restore lost colors!

He lost his bright colors because of a recent enchanted rain.

Will you help him become beautiful and colorful again?

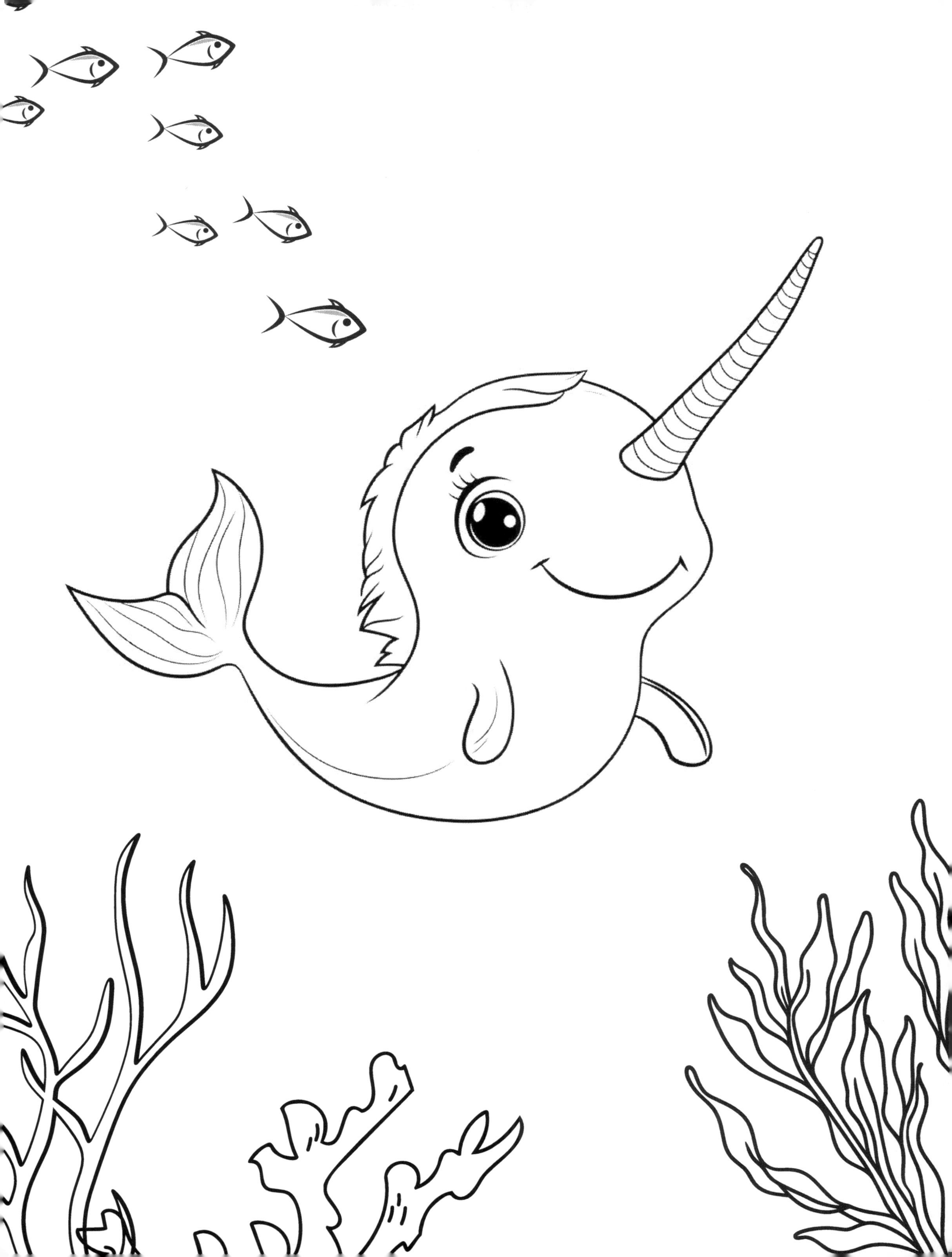

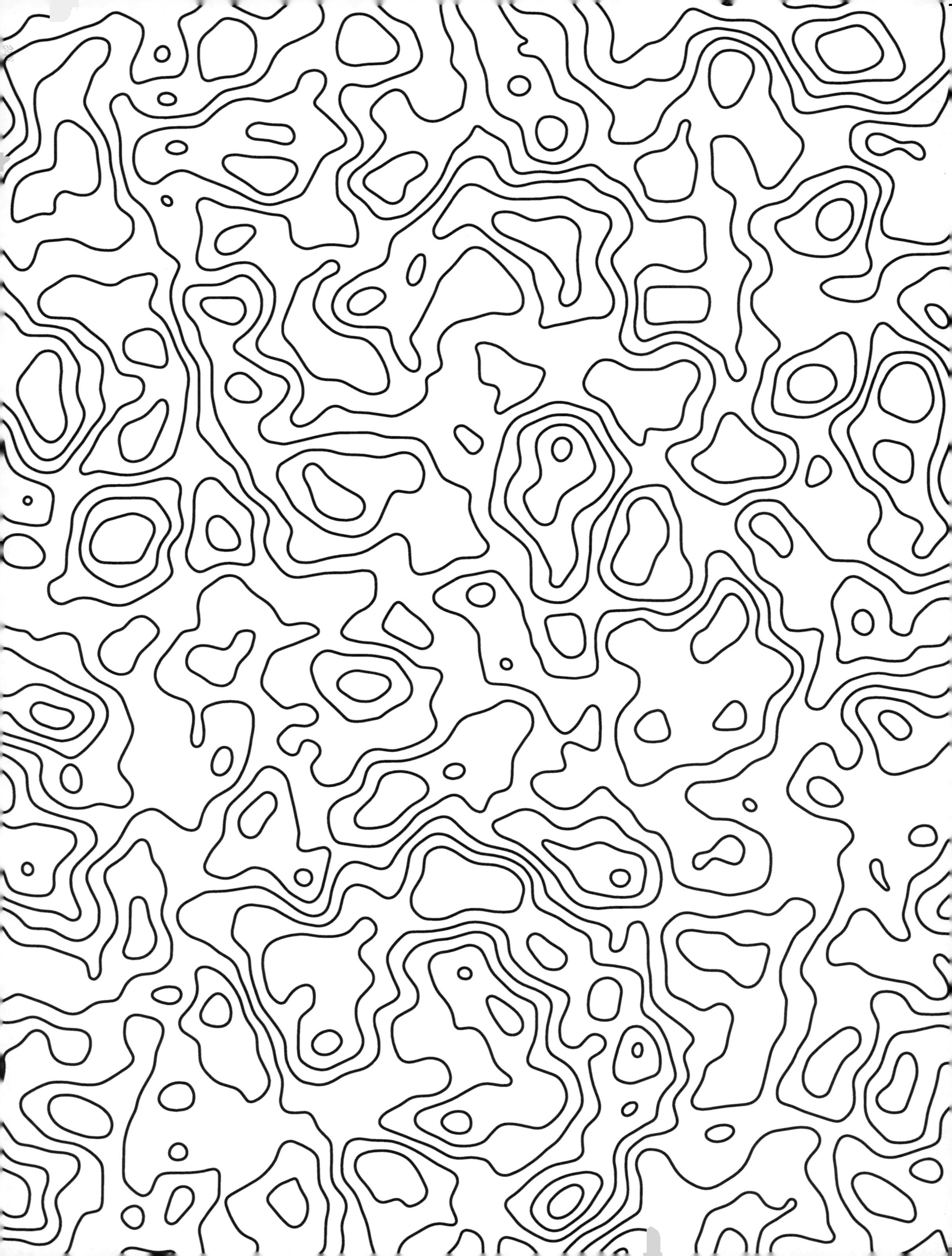

O OWL

Owls are special birds that stay awake at night. They can see in the dark better than most other animals.

Owls have a cool trick—they can turn their heads almost all the way around!

O

Now, my little friend, let's try to write the letter 'O'. Are you ready?

O O O
_____

_____

_____

This owl is usually brightly colored. Yesterday, she flew with her friend, the eagle, who told her about your magical colors.

The owl really wants to get her colors back, which were washed away by the magic rain!

Will you help her?

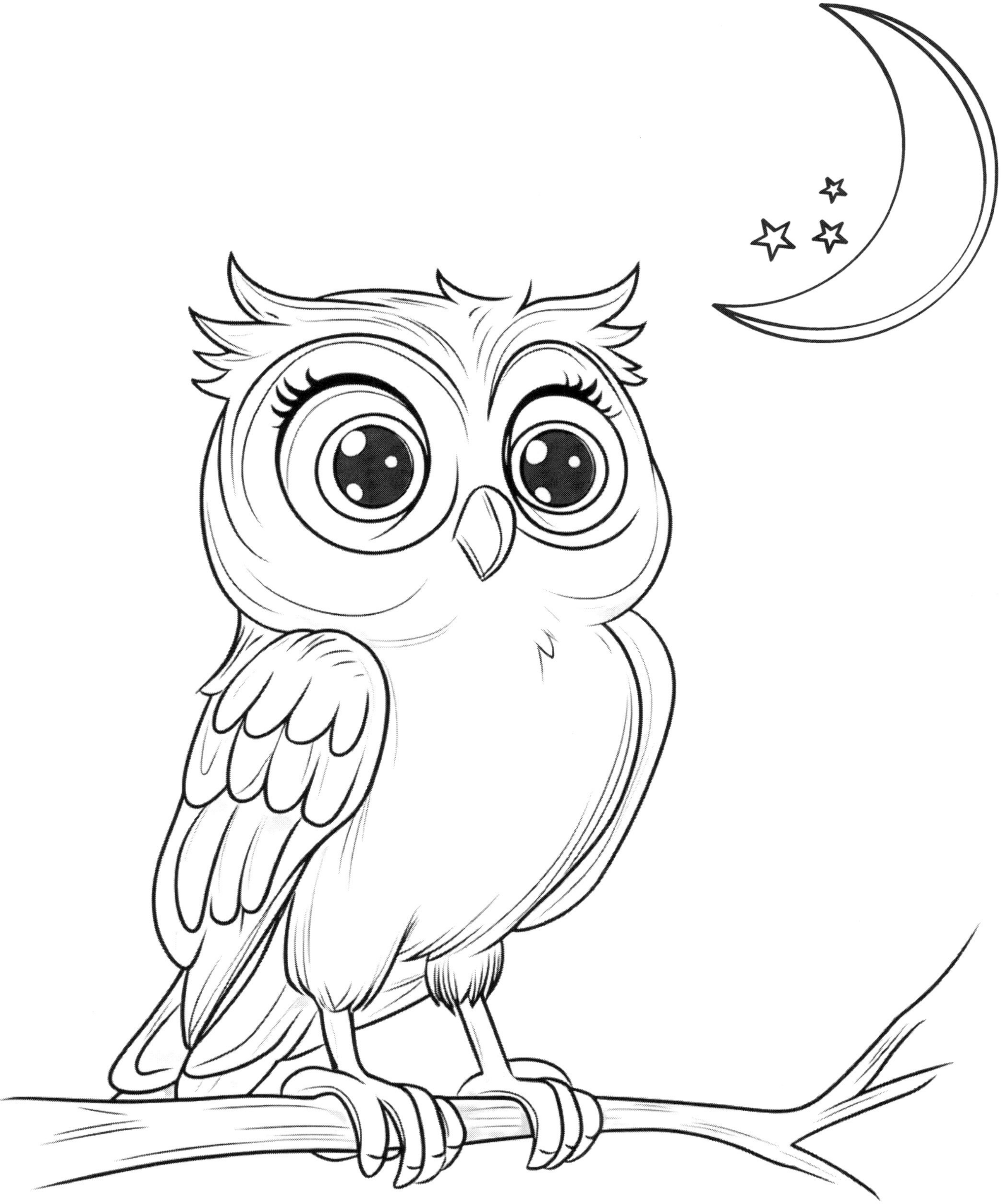

P PENGUIN

Penguins live in cold places with lots of ice and constant frost. They can swim very fast. They have short wings that they use like flippers.

Penguins have their own daycares. When most of the adults go off to find food, a few stay behind as caretakers to watch over the young ones.

P

Well, my little friend, let's give writing the letter 'P' a try!
Are you excited?

P P P _____

_____

_____

My little friend, a new visitor has come to see you! It's a penguin, and he's asking you to use your magic to help him become colorful.

What do you say, can you help him?

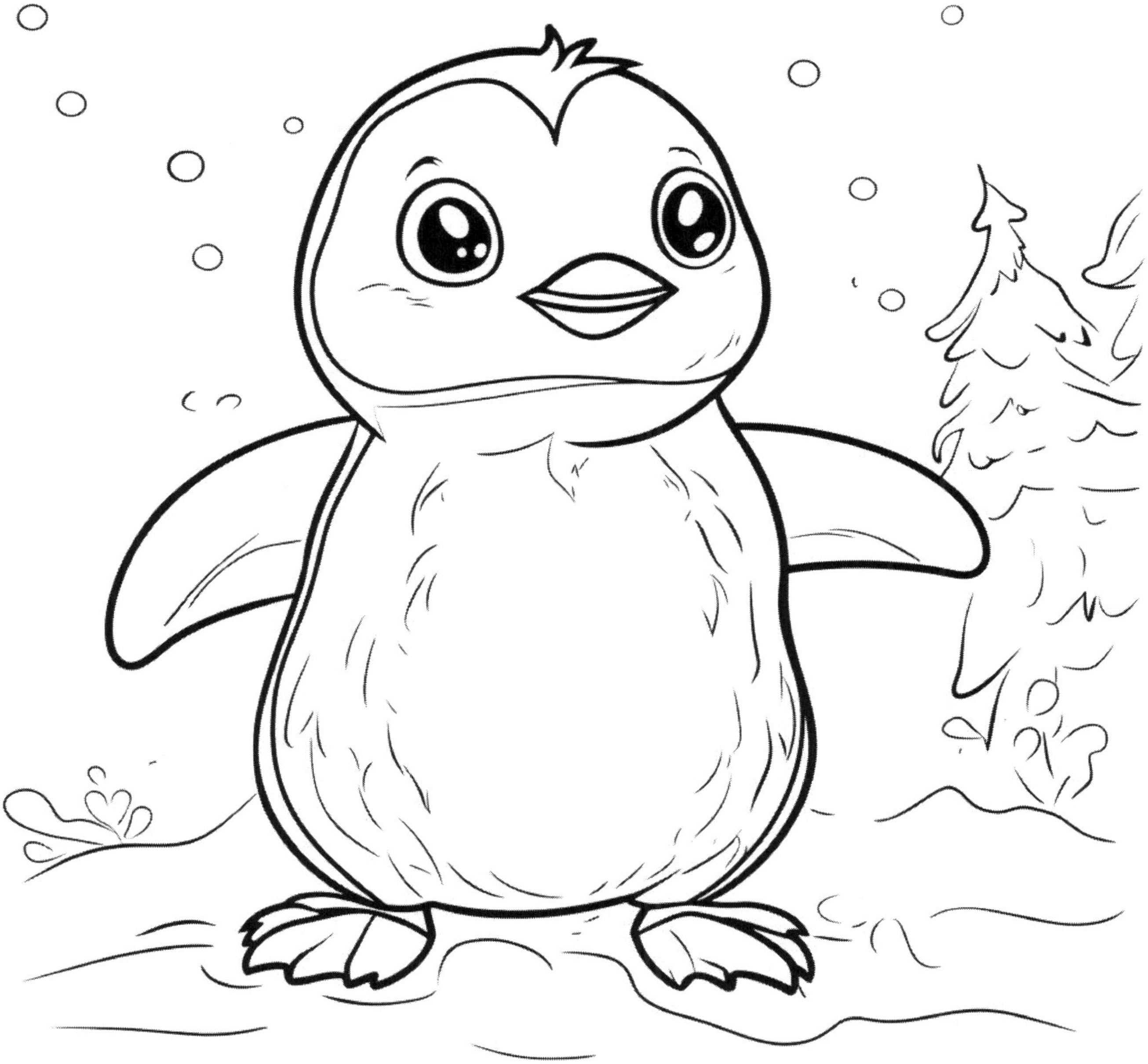

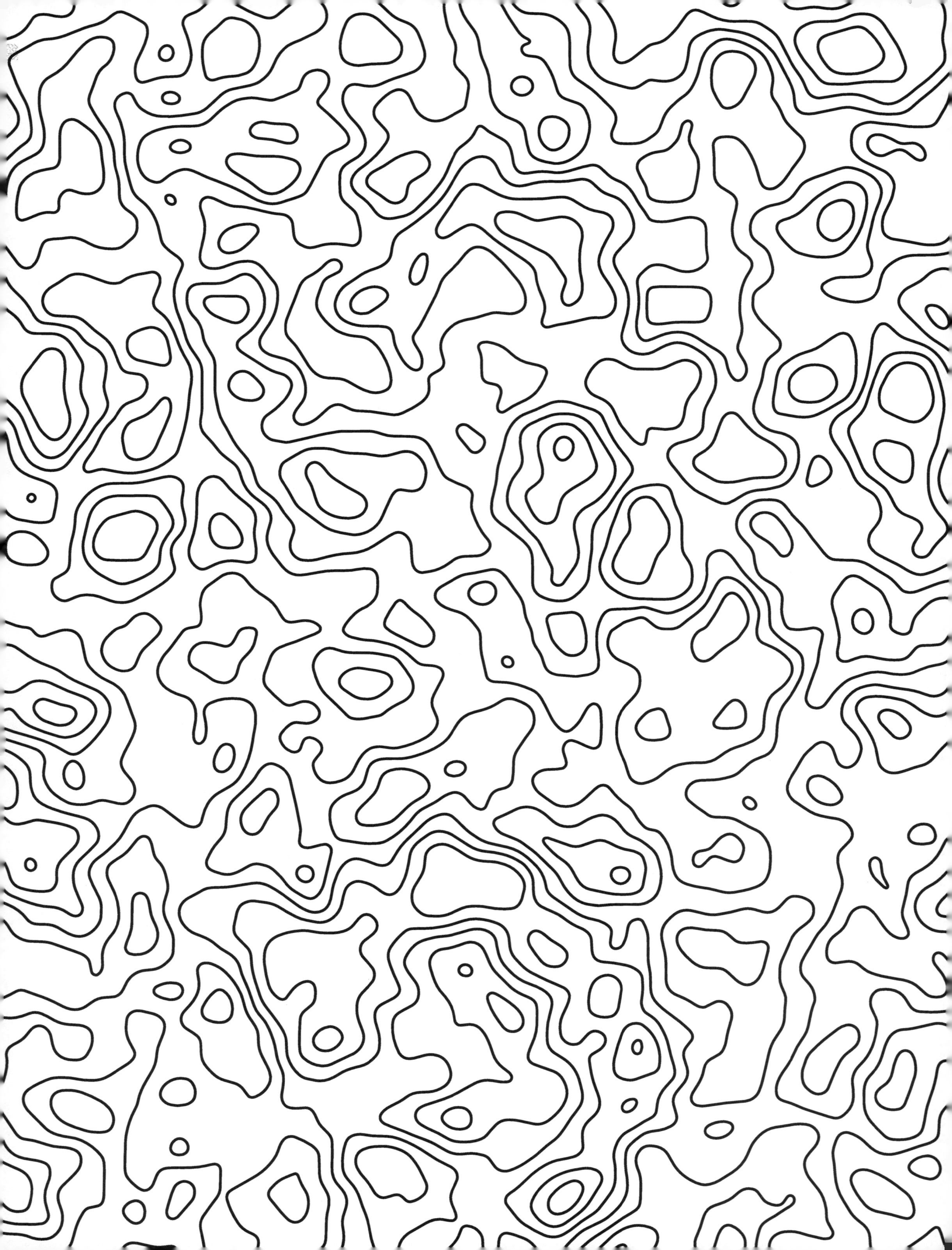

Q

QUOKKA

Quokkas always look like they're smiling.

Due to the shape of their faces, quokkas have a constant expression that resembles
a smile, which is why they are called 'the happiest animals in the world.'

Quokkas are found only in Australia.

Q

Okay, my little friend, let's practice writing the letter 'Q' together! Ready to start?

Q Q Q

_____

_____

_____

Look how this quokka is smiling at you! I think she likes you! She wants you to like her too, but she's a little shy because the rain has turned her black and white.

Would you like to help her?

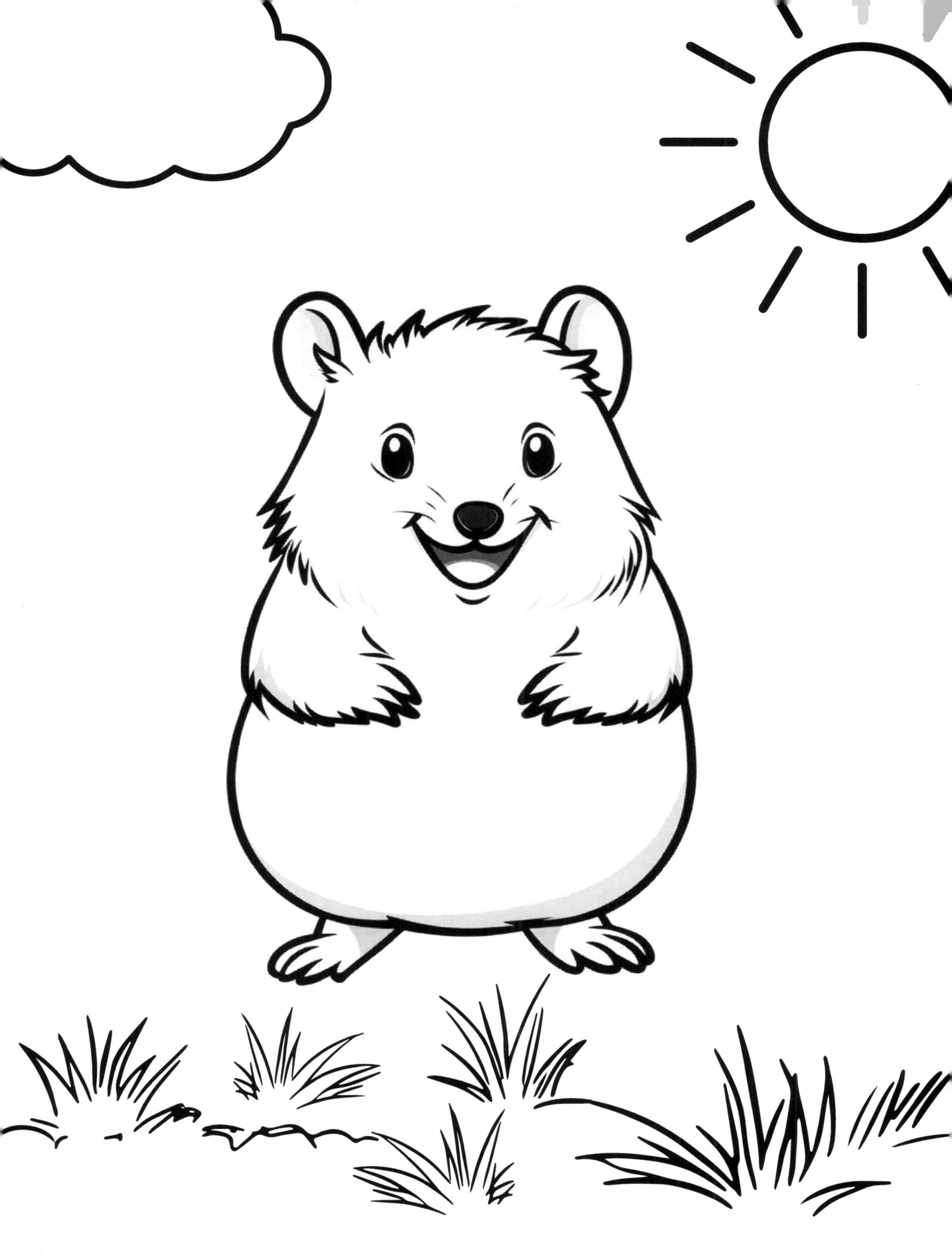

R RABBIT

Rabbits are great jumpers. They can cover up to 10 feet in a single leap!

Plus, their large eyes help them see almost everything around them, even from behind!

Rabbits also love being with friends, so they like to live in big groups.

R

Alright, my little friend, let's give writing the letter 'R' a try!
Are you excited?

R R R _____

_____

_____

This rabbit is very sad because he was just recently brown, and now he's colorless. My little friend, we simply must help him!

Let's make this poor fellow happy again!

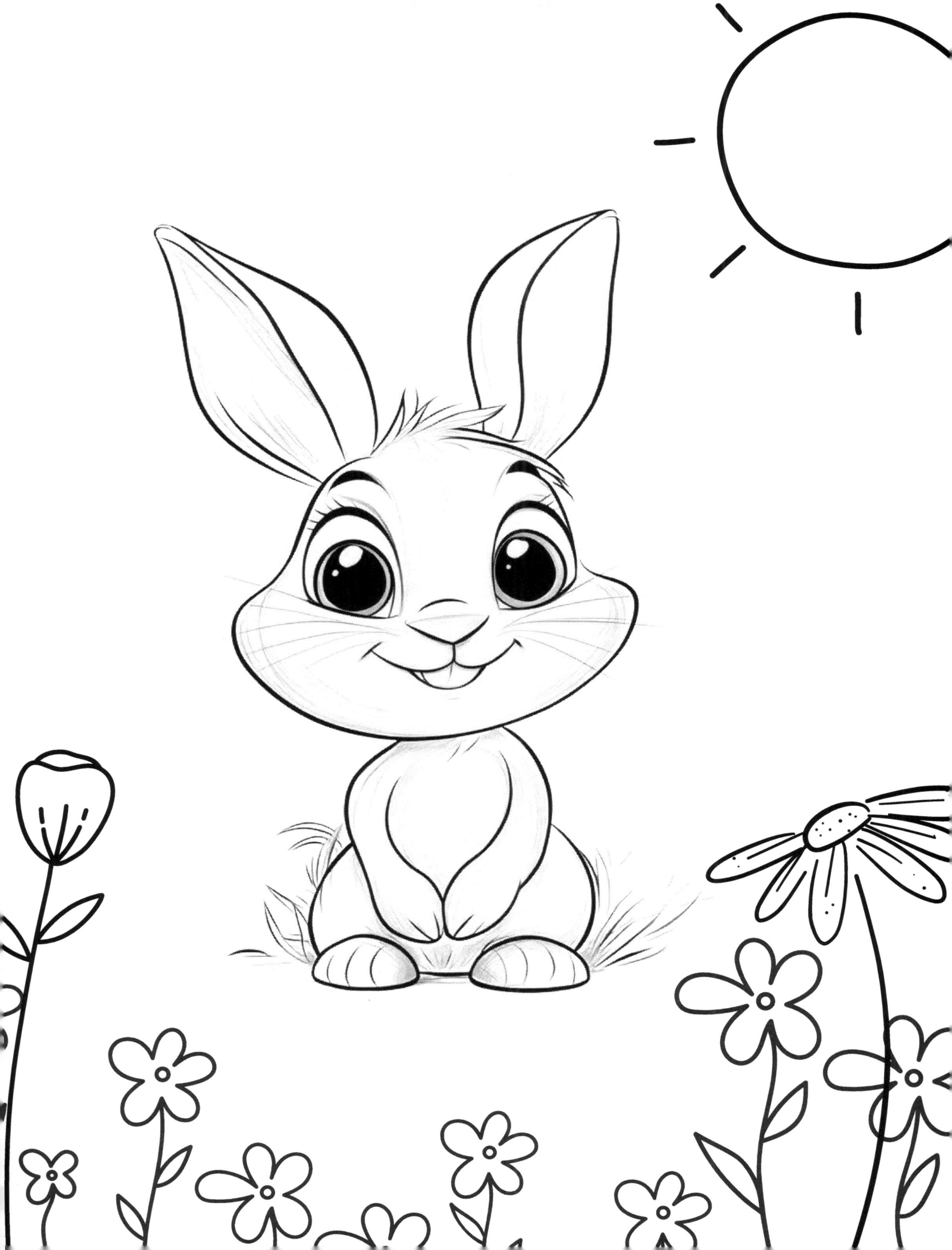

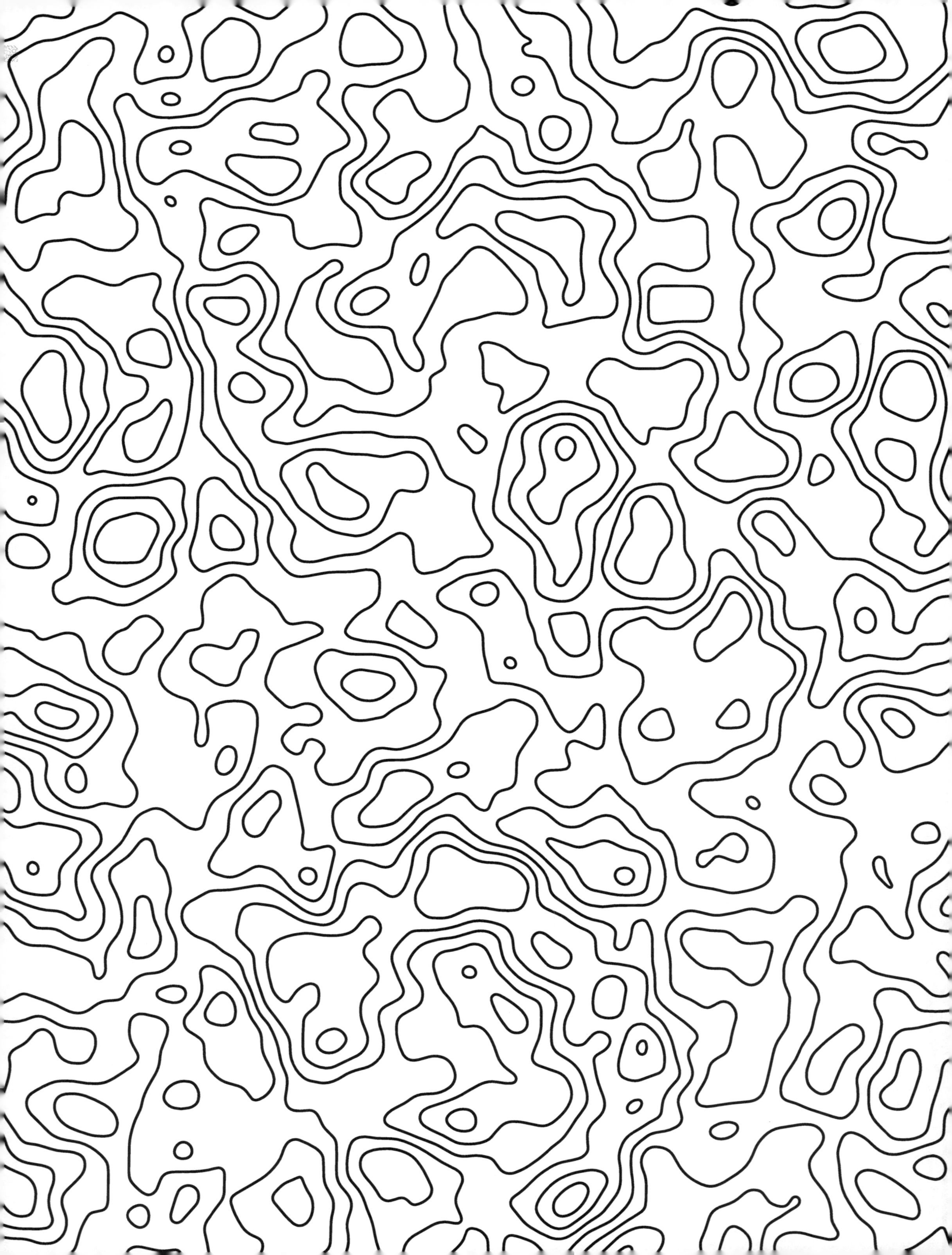

S SNAKE

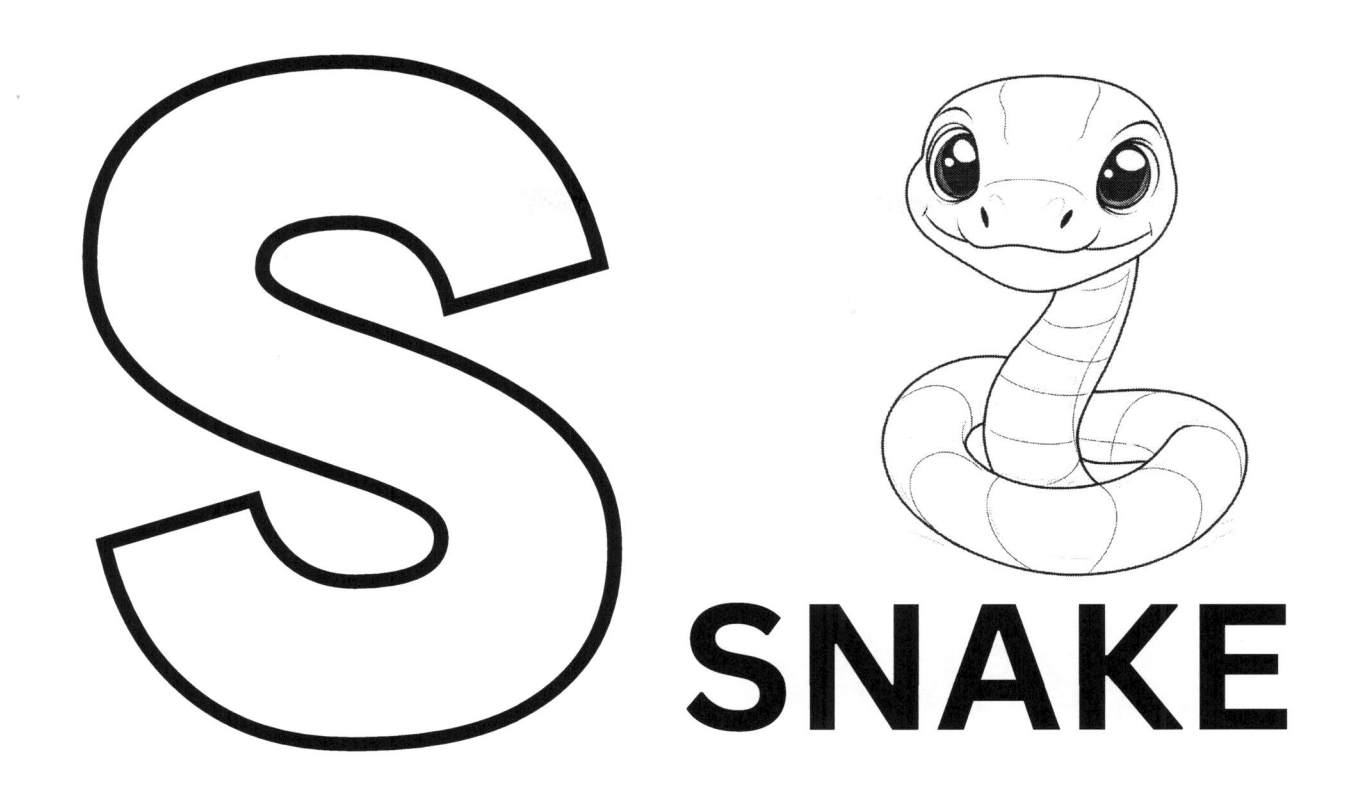

Snakes are amazing creatures that can be tiny, like a pencil, or as long as a bus. They move without legs—they slither on their bellies!

Many snakes lay eggs as birds, and some can 'fly,' covering short distances between trees. Snakes don't have ears, but they feel little shakes in the ground to "hear."

There are dangerous snakes whose venom can be deadly, but most are totally safe and won't hurt people.

S

Now, my little friend, let's try to write the letter 'S'. Are you ready?

S S S

This kind snake has waited a long time for its turn to meet you.

What colors should we choose for it?

Only you can help solve this issue, my little friend!

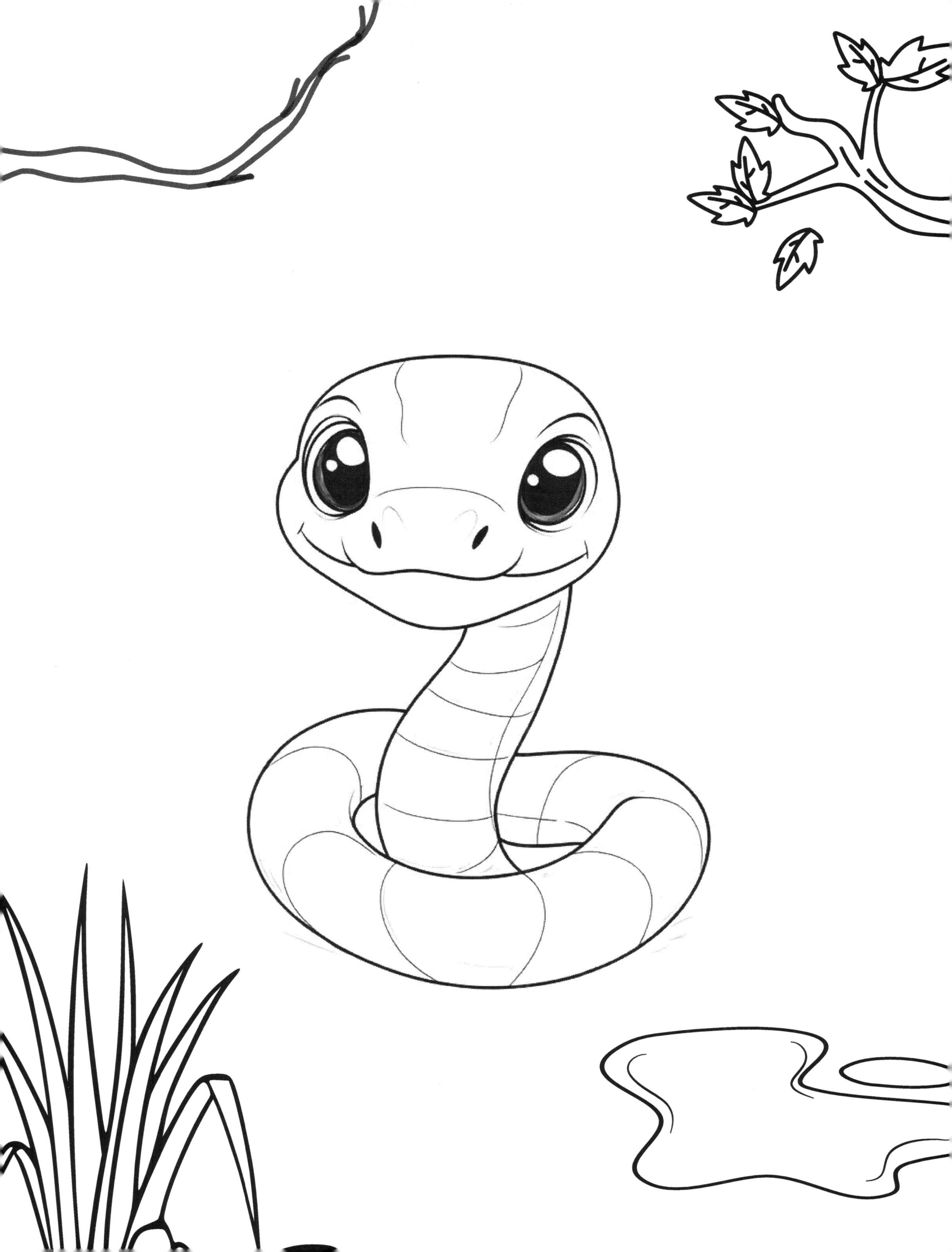

T TURTLE

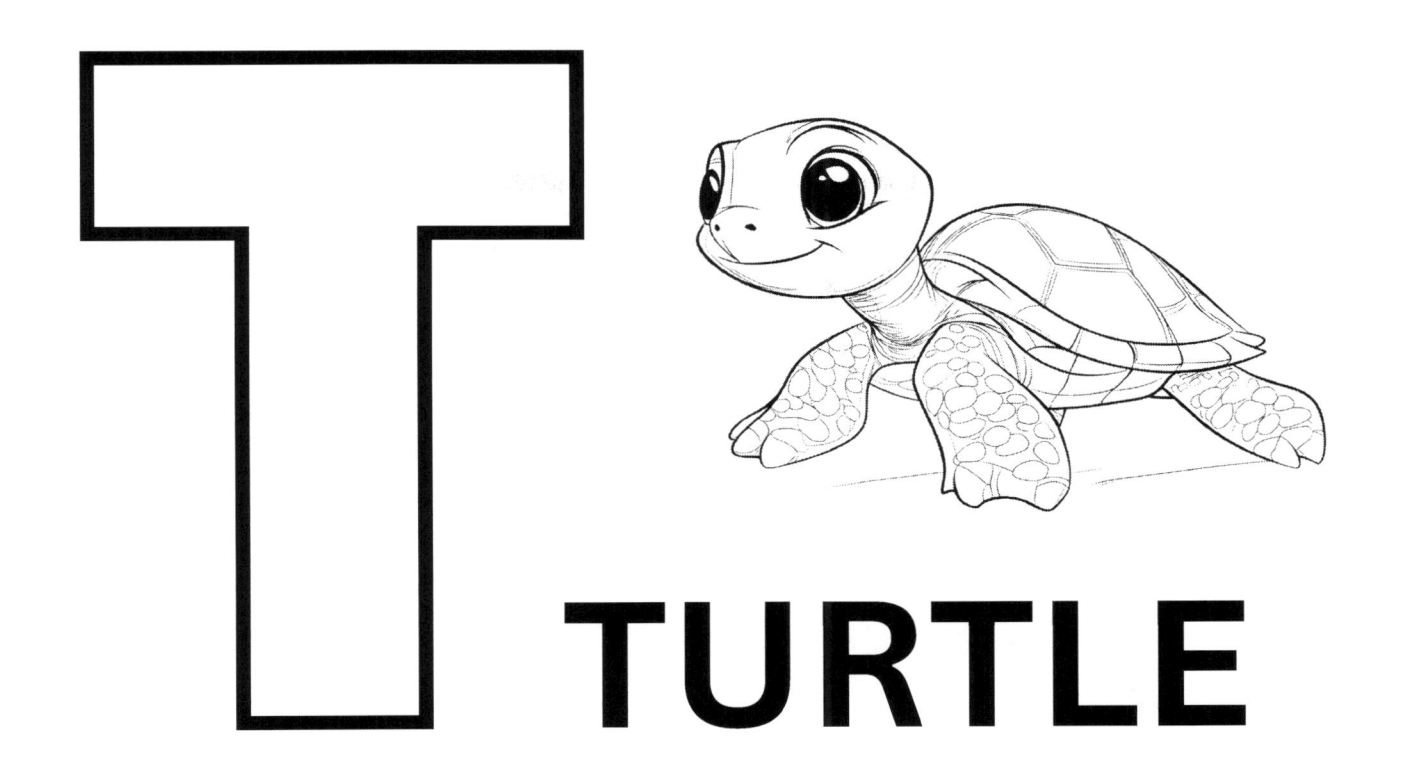

Turtles live very long lives. Some can live up to 200 years.

They have a hard shell that protects them from predators.

Turtles walk slowly, but they are good swimmers.

T

Okay, my little friend, let's practice writing the letter 'T' together! Ready to start?

T T T

Pigmentikus's dark magic has affected this little turtle too. She heard that you can help.

Want to give it a try?

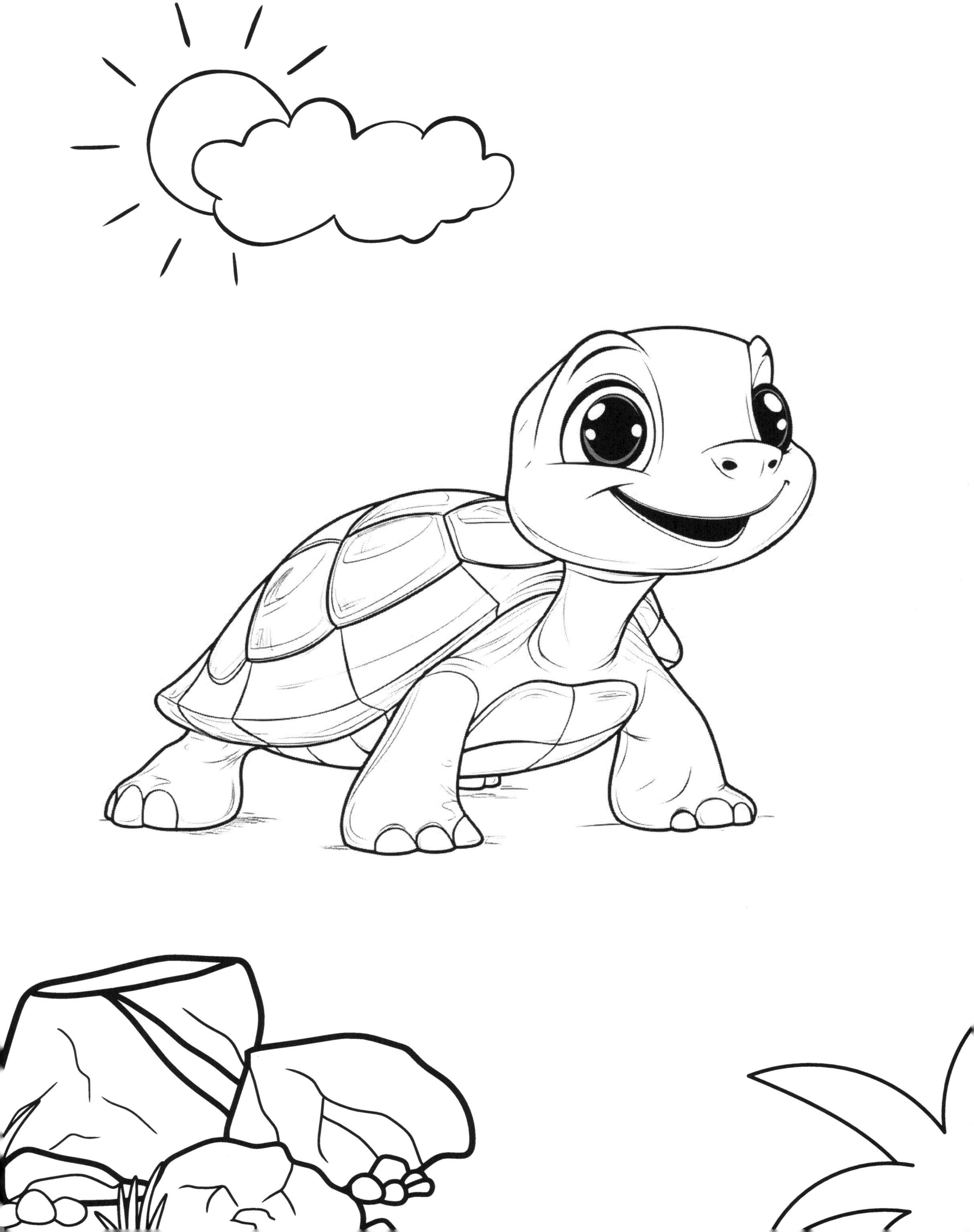

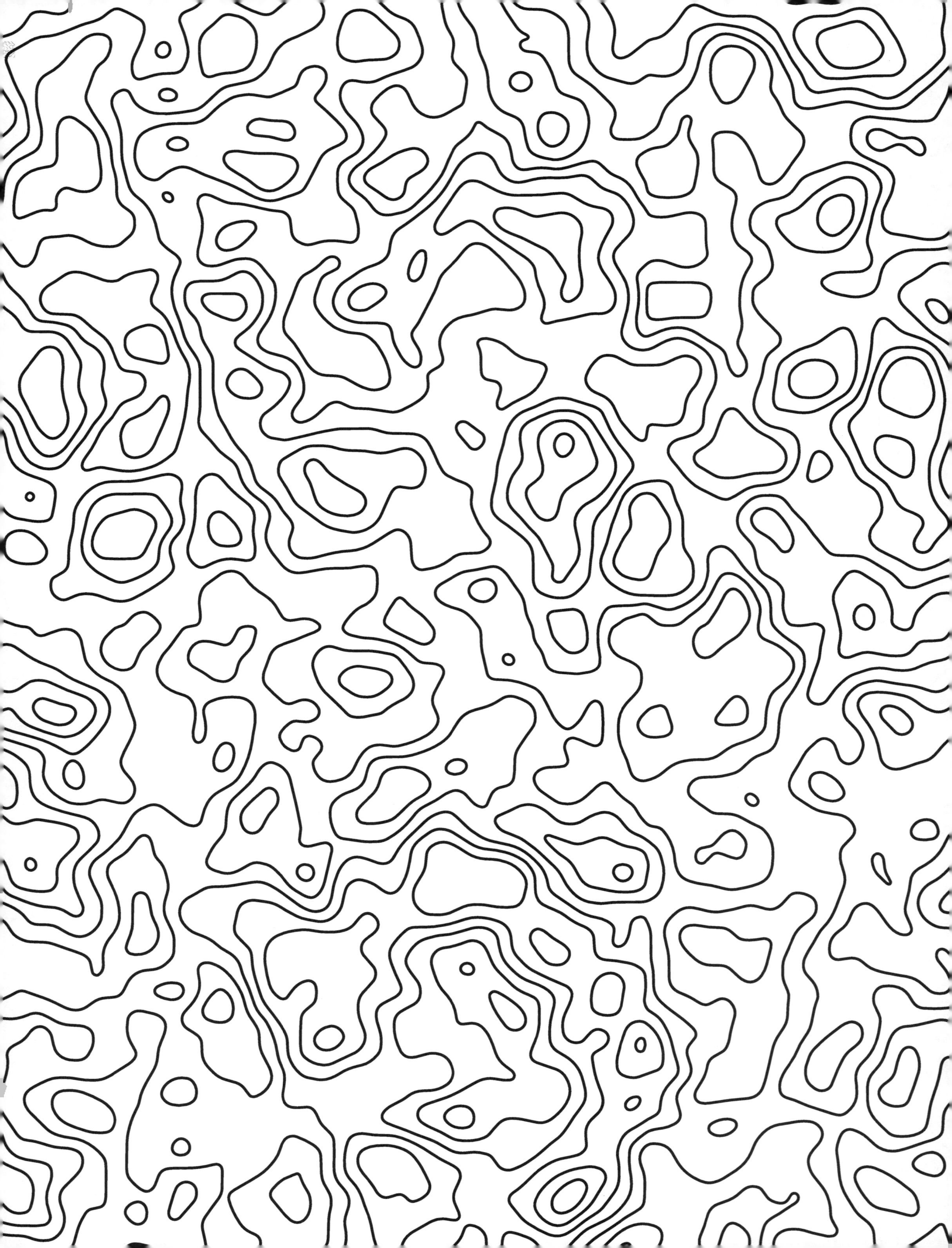

Urchin

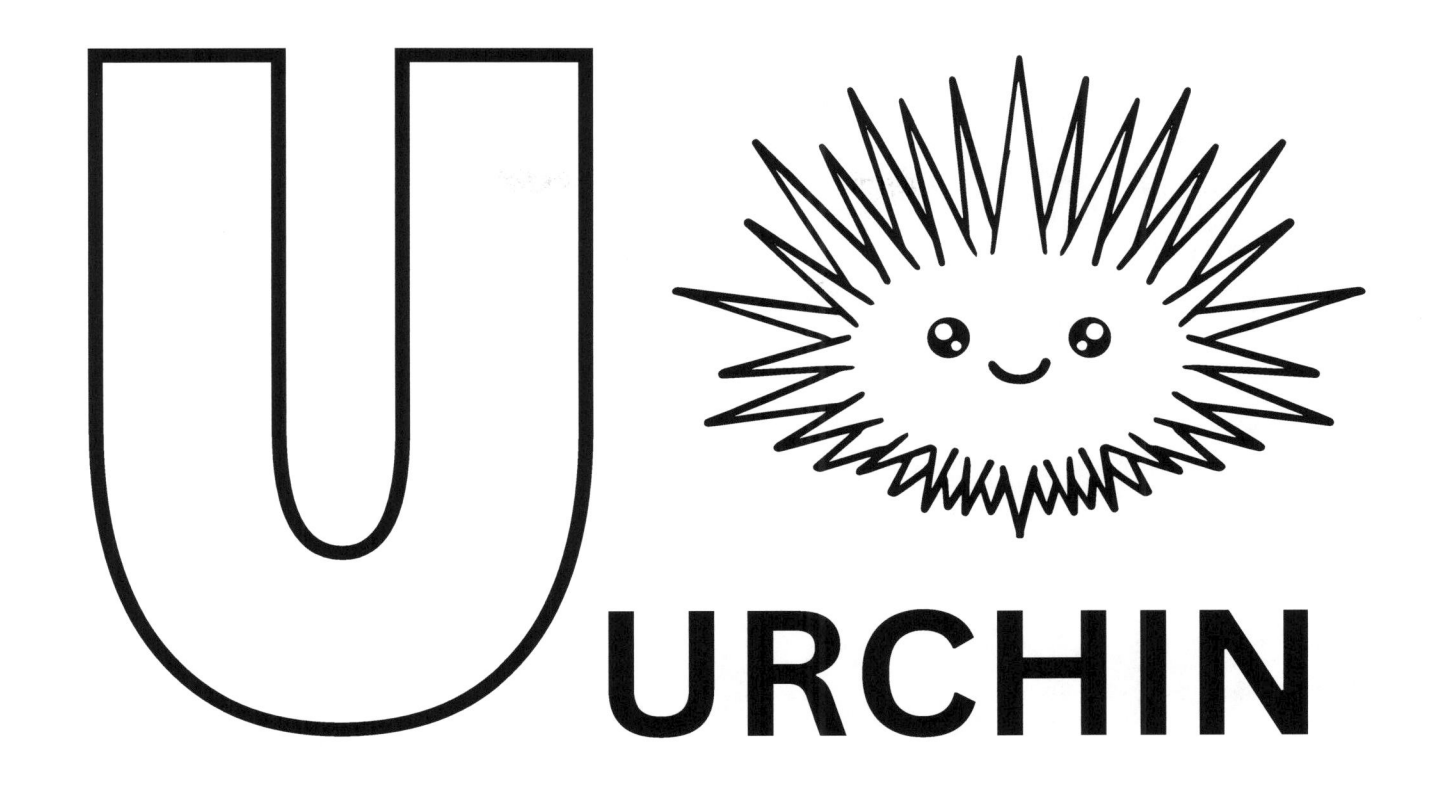

Sea urchins are small marine creatures covered in spines that help protect them from predators.

They crawl along the ocean floor using their spines and love to hide among rocks. Each sea urchin has its own unique pattern of spines, and they can come in a variety of colors!

U

Alright, my little friend, let's give writing the letter 'U' a try!

Are you excited?

U U U _____

_____

_____

This sea urchin is a friend of the turtle. The turtle told him how great you are and how well you can use your magic wands.

What colors do you think would make our new friend beautiful and protected?

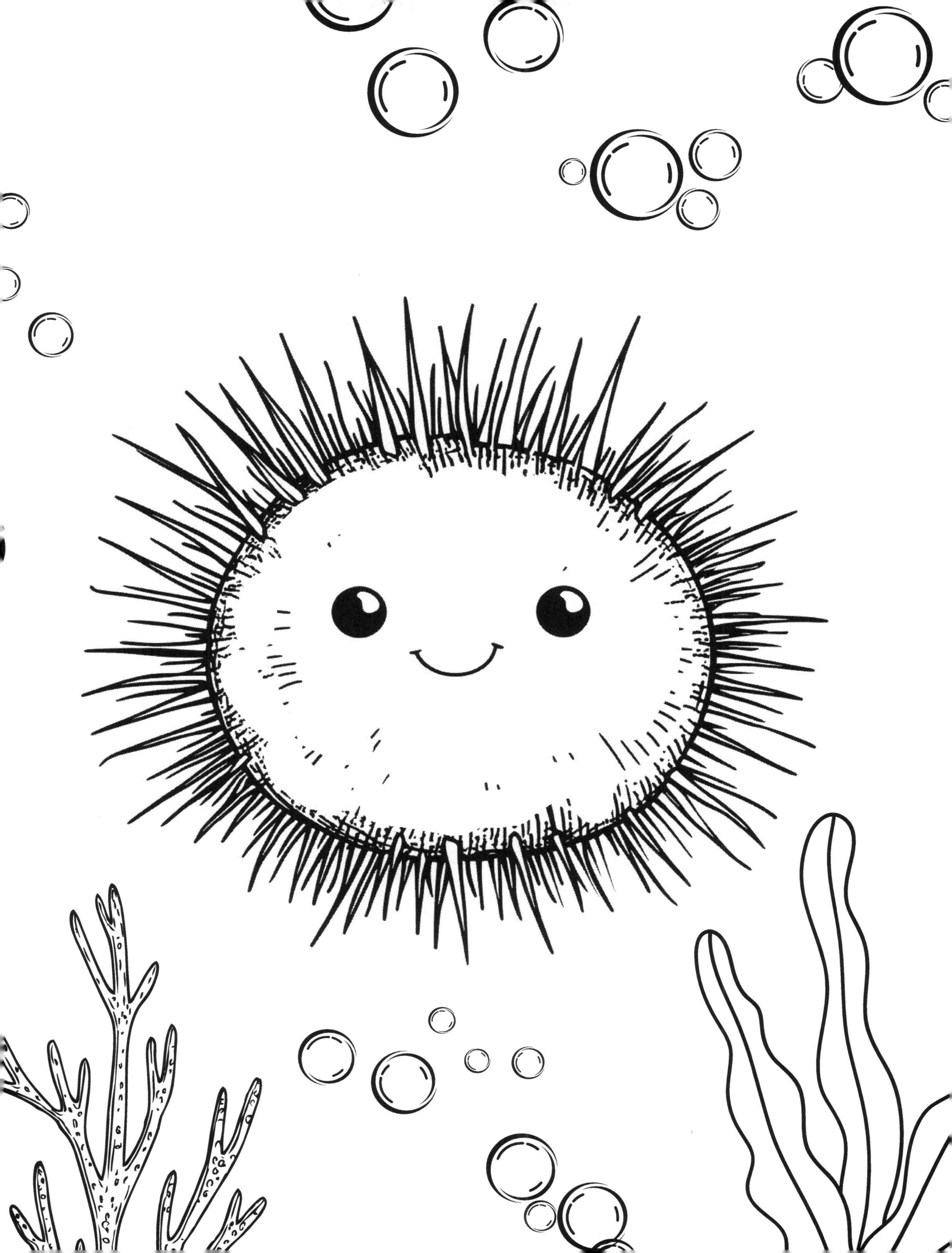

V

VULTURE

Vultures help nature stay clean by eating animals that are no longer alive. That prevents the spread of diseases.

Thanks to their large wings, vultures can soar in the air for hours without flapping.

Vultures also have excellent long-distance vision, almost as good as eagles.

V

*Alright, my little friend, let's give writing the letter 'V' a try!
Are you excited?*

V V V

This vulture really wants to have bright feathers to amaze his friends. He heard that you're wonderful at coloring!

Will you help him?

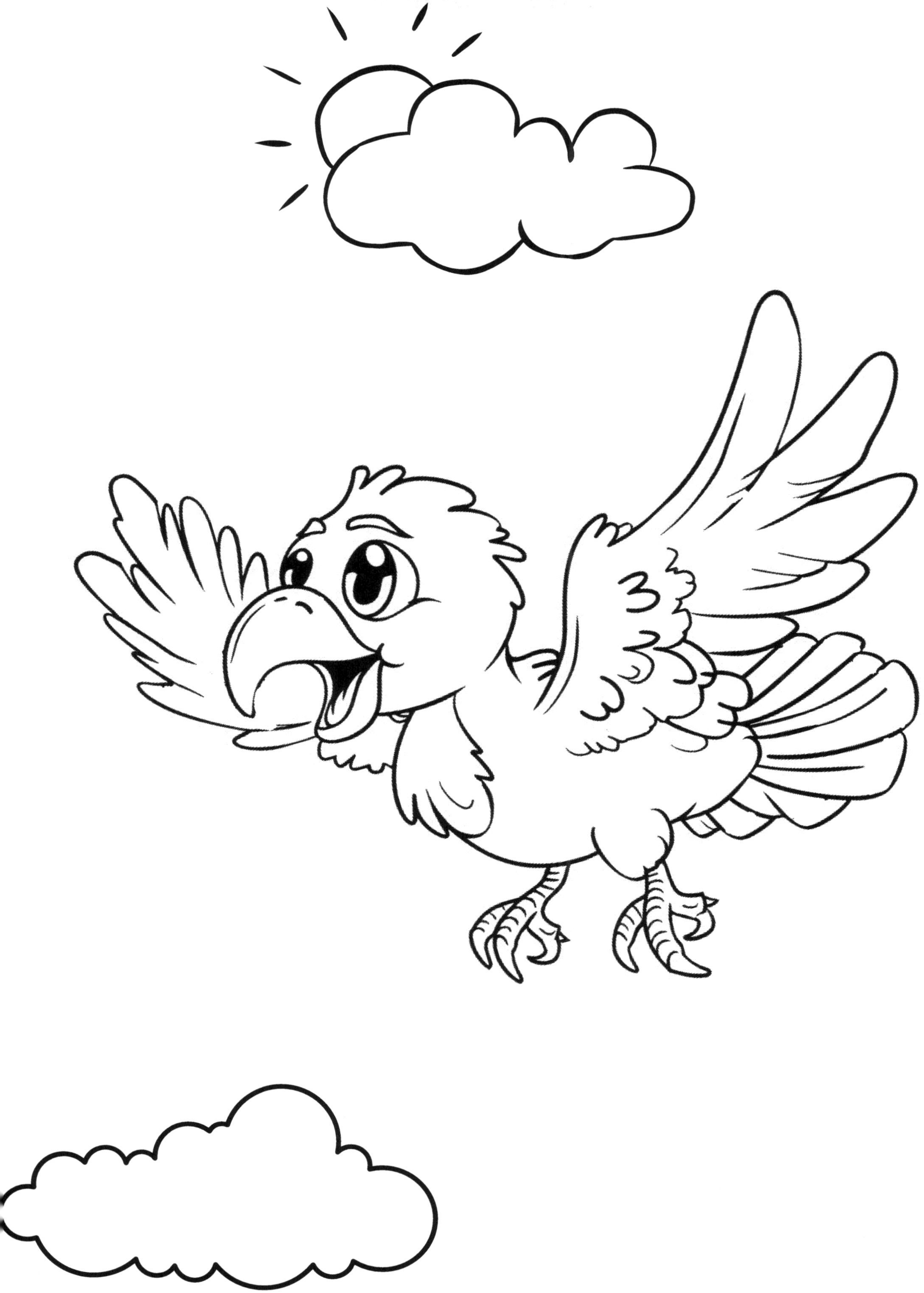

W
WALRUS

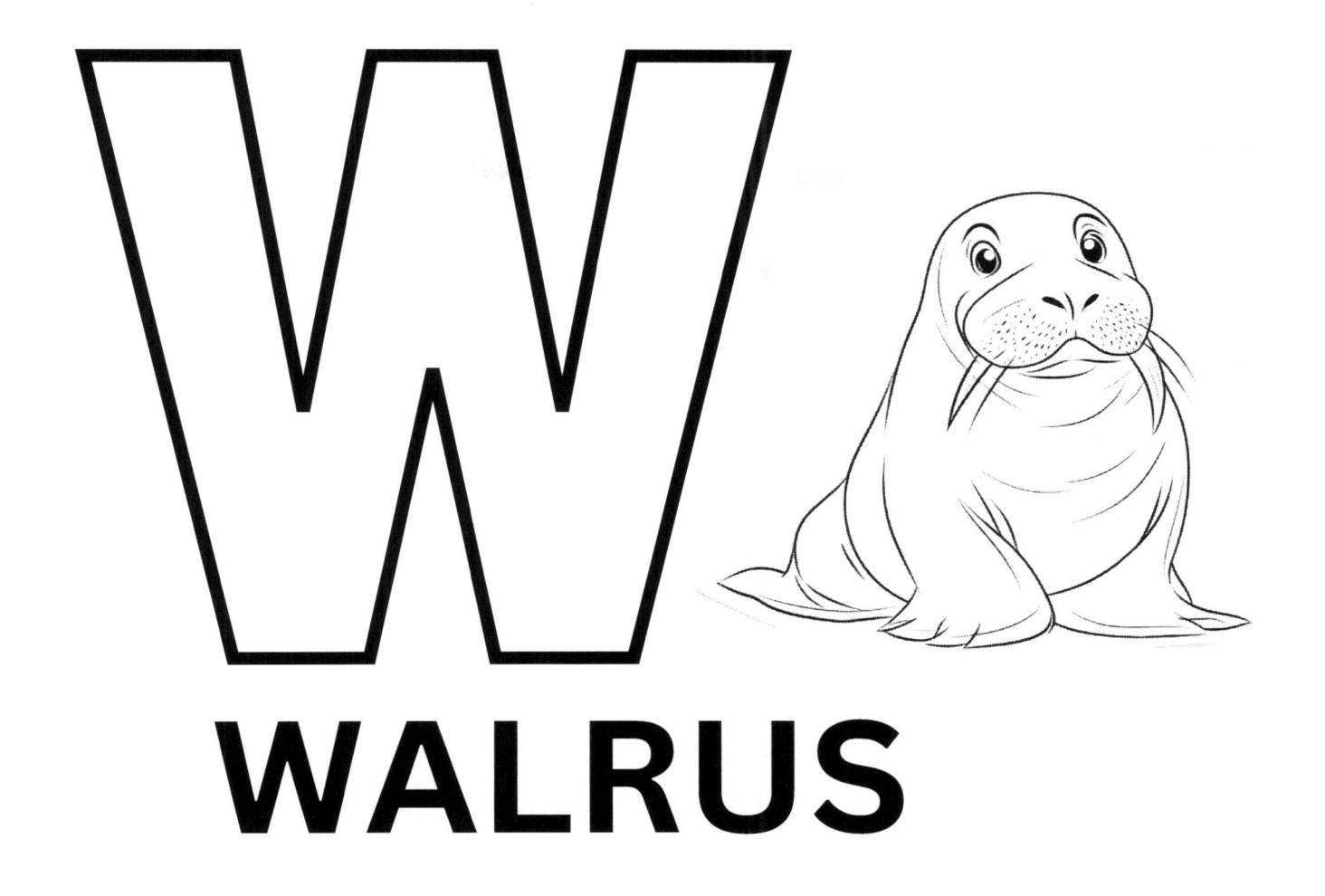

Walruses are large sea animals with long tusks. Their thick skin and fat help them stay warm in cold water.

Walruses can grow very big—longer than a car and as heavy as two big trucks!

They love to rest in big groups, lying on ice like they're at the beach.

W

*Now, my little friend, let's try to write the letter 'W'.
Are you ready?*

W W W
_____

_____

_____

This smiling walrus was very beautiful before the rain, and now he really needs your magic.

Please help him get his colors back — he will be very grateful to you!

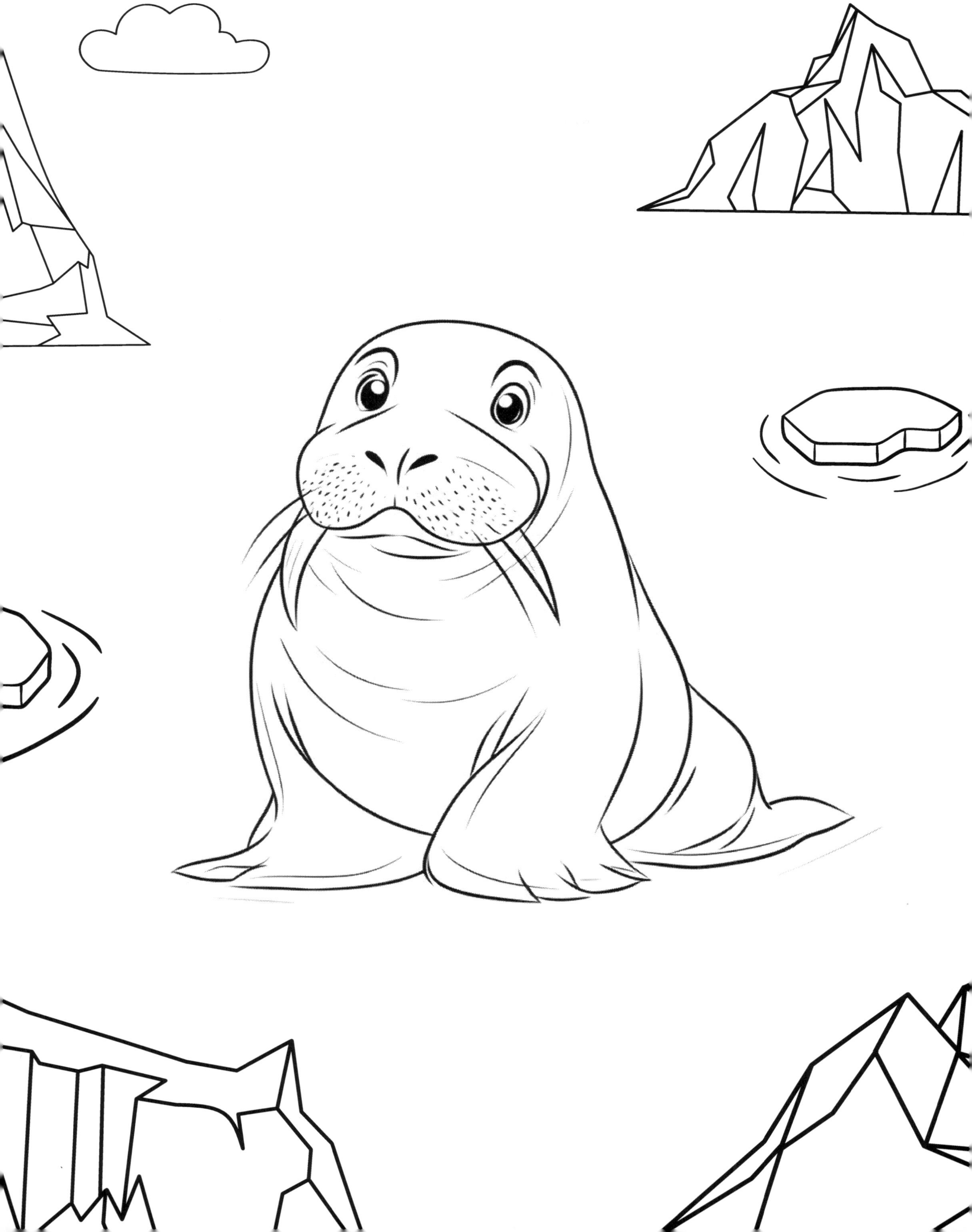

X

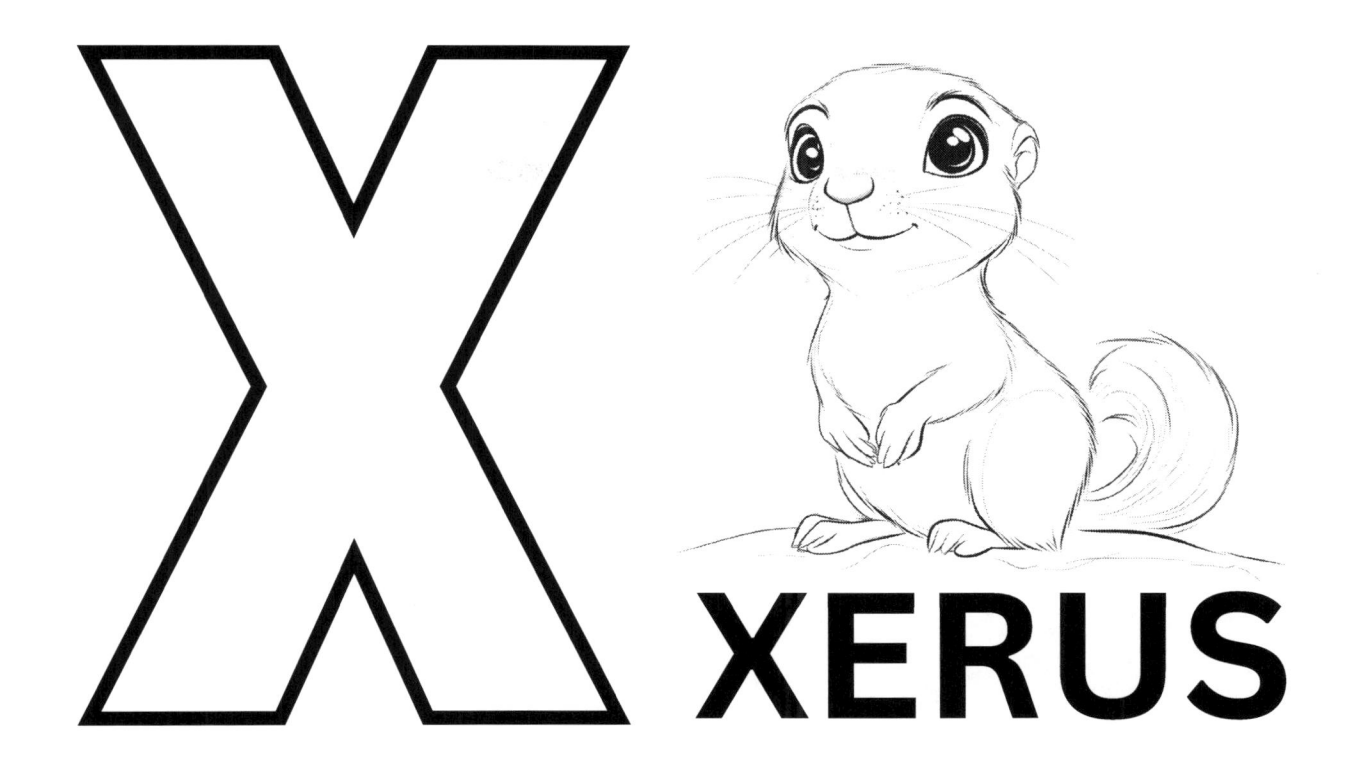

XERUS

The xeruses are ground squirrels that live in the deserts of Africa. They build huge and long tunnels underground, which helps them escape the heat and hide from predators.

They have large fluffy tails, which they use like an umbrella to shield themselves from the sun.

X

*Well, my little friend, now let's write the letter 'X' together!
Ready to start?*

X X X _____

_____

_____

Just a little more, and all the animals on the island will be colorful and happy again!

This xerus has come for your help!

Would you like to color him?

Y YAK

Yaks are big, fluffy animals that live in cold, high mountains. They have long, shaggy hair to keep them warm and big horns to help dig through snow for food.

Yaks love to eat grass and flowers, and they make a funny grunting sound, like "gruuunnnt!"

People use yaks to carry heavy things and make butter and cheese from their milk.

They're like super helpers in the mountains!

Y

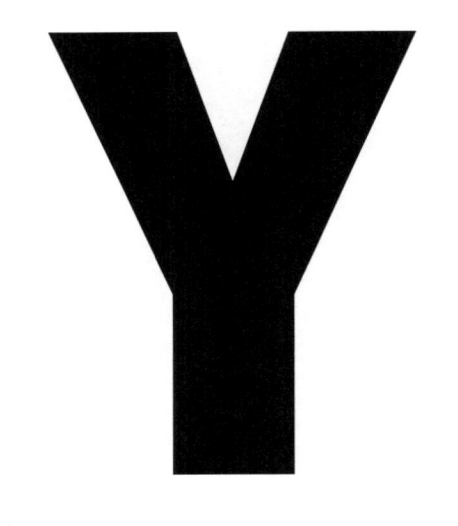

Now, my little friend, let's try to write the letter 'Y'. Are you ready?

Y Y Y _____

_____

_____

This yak wants to be bright so he can stand out in the snowy mountains.

Will you help him become beautiful?

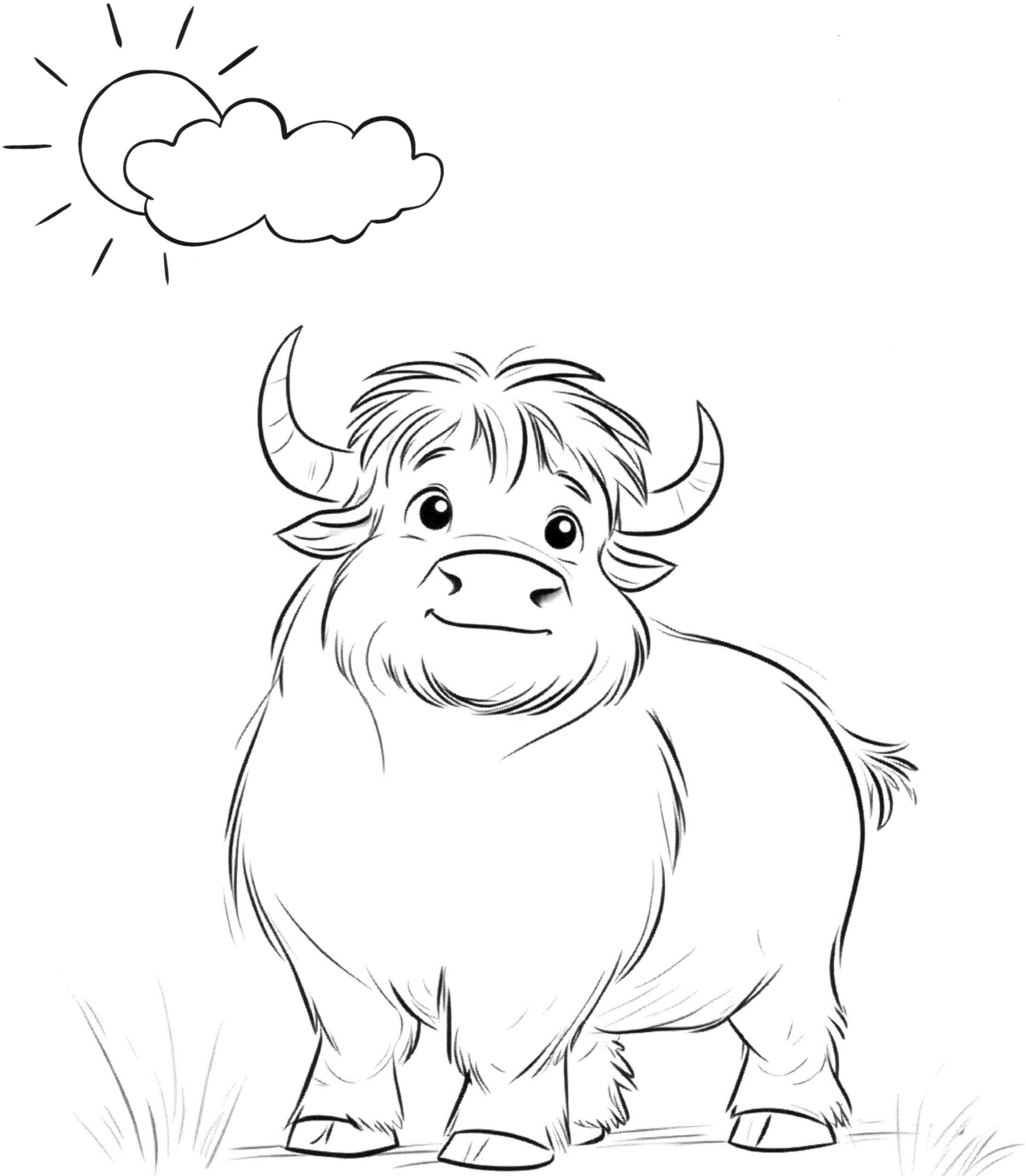

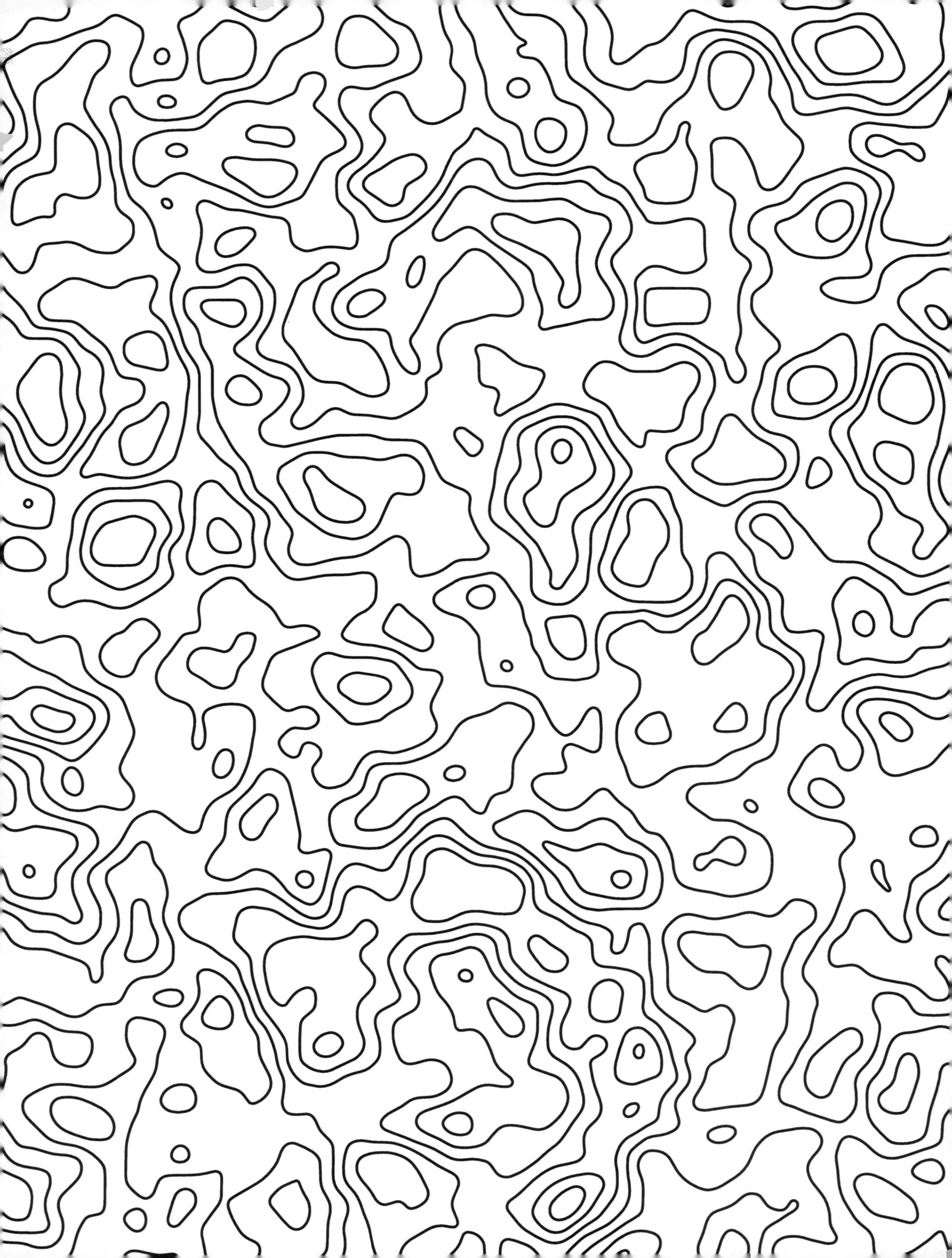

Z ZEBRA

Zebras are animals with cool black-and-white stripes! They have amazing eyesight - they can even see in the dark!

Did you know zebras are super fast runners? They can zoom as fast as 40 miles an hour, like a race car! And zebras don't just neigh and snort like horses - they can bark too! It is so funny!

Z

Now, my little friend, let's try to write the letter 'W'. Are you ready?

Z Z Z _____

_____

_____

This zebra got caught in Pigmentikus's rain, and her stripes washed away! She wants you to help her get her stripes back.

Will you help the zebra become beautiful again?

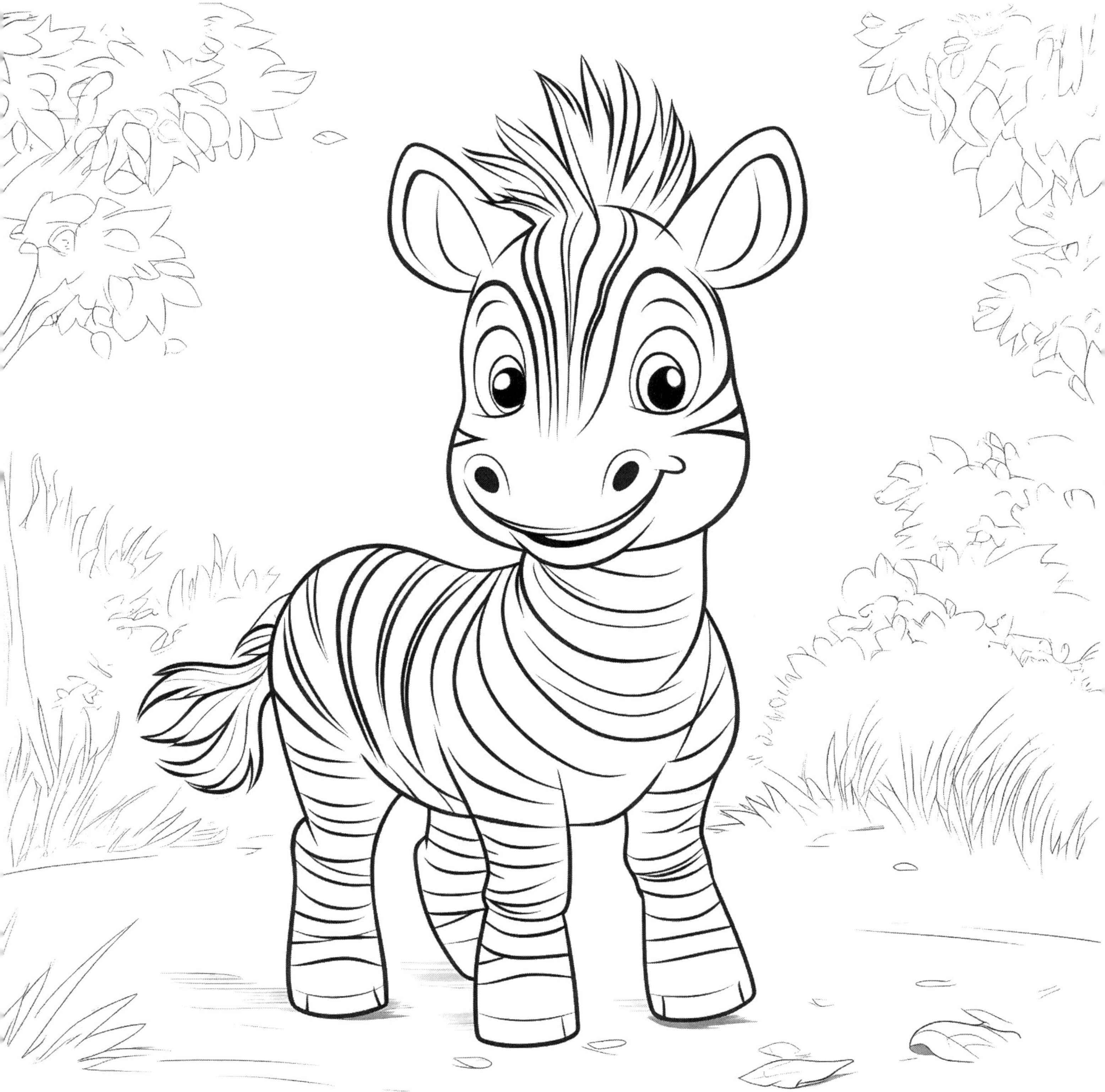

Now all the animals are happy again!

But the wizard Pigmentikus is still on the island. We could banish him, but he has nowhere else to go.

So, we will let him stay on our island, but take away his magical powers so that he can no longer harm anyone!

To do this, you need to recite a magic colorful spell!

Say out loud:

COLORS, REURN!

That's it! The wizard is no longer a threat!

When Pigmentikus lost his magic, he felt sad.

But don't worry, his sadness didn't last long. Now he has made friends with everyone on our magical island and is very happy that you helped him become a kind!

You've done an amazing job, and I congratulate you!

Well done!!!

AUTHOR'S NOTE:

If you and your child enjoyed this coloring book, please leave a review on Amazon.

It means so much to me!

Thank you, and see you next time.

Made in United States
Orlando, FL
28 February 2025